The Primary Comprehension Toolkit
Language and Lessons for Active Literacy

Stephanie Harvey & Anne Goudvis

Teacher's Guide

Dedication: *To Smokey Daniels—our editor extraordinaire, thoughtful colleague, and good friend.*
We're thrilled that you channel our thinking so clearly and keep us laughing along the way.

Photography: David Stirling, Mason Jones, Smokey Daniels, David Johnson

The authors and publisher wish to thank those who have generously given permission to reprint borrowed materials.

Post-its ® are a registered trademark of the 3M Company

Library of Congress Cataloging-in-Publication Data
CIP data on file with the Library of Congress

The Primary Comprehension Toolkit Teacher's Guide
ISBN-13: 978-0-325-02154-6, ISBN-10: 0-325-02154-6

The Primary Comprehension Toolkit: Language and Lessons for Active Literacy
ISBN-13: 978-0-325-00997-1,   ISBN-10: 0-325-00997-X

Printed in the United States of America on acid-free paper
12 11 10 09 08 ML 1 2 3 4 5

firsthand
HEINEMANN

firsthand
An imprint of Heinemann
361 Hanover Street
Portsmouth, NH 03801-3912
firsthand.heinemann.com
Offices and agents throughout the world

Acknowledgments

The Primary Comprehension Toolkit was a team effort in every sense of the word. In fact, all of the team should be listed on the cover as authors! But practicality prevails, so instead we acknowledge them here.

The *Toolkit* wouldn't have happened without the creative energy, enthusiasm, and unwavering support of Leigh Peake and Smokey Daniels. We marvel at their understanding of and vision for this resource.

*First*hand's *Toolkit* Team—Jean Lawler, Tina Miller, Charles McQuillen, David Stirling, Heather Anderson, Stephanie Levy, Deb Eaton, and Steve Bernier—kept us on track and worked tirelessly to make *Toolkit* the best it could be while never losing their senses of humor. We are truly grateful for all they have done for us.

Kelley Hersey, Ed Stevens, Karen Jones, and Jenny Greenleaf developed an outstanding design that gives *Toolkit* its sense of unity and brings all the pieces together in a stunningly beautiful way.

Pip Clews and The Troupe created the wonderful DVD-ROM, which is jam-packed with amazing offerings. The people at RT Productions captured our teaching and kids' learning on video so that teachers can really see what Active Literacy looks like. David Stirling, Mason Jones, Smokey Daniels, and David Johnson took the gorgeous photographs that bring *The Primary Toolkit* to life.

And a huge thanks to Lesa Scott who brought this whole team together.

A special thanks to the wonderful teachers who opened their classrooms to us throughout this project—Brad Buhrow, Anne Upczak Garcia, Jennifer Shouse, Sue Kempton, Lynne Albert, Marisol Payet, Kristen Elder-Rubino, and Barb Smith. They have created classrooms that are truly magical places for learning. Librarians Nell Box and Melissa Oviatt collaborated with us to try out and refine primary research practices. Many thanks to Lynn Widger, the principal of Columbine Elementary in Boulder, Colorado, who welcomed us daily with open arms and a smile. And to Liz Stedem, our longtime friend and colleague, who once again helped us discover some of the hidden treasures that appear on our trade book bibliography. Thank you!

The beautiful faces and work that appear throughout the *Toolkit* belong to some of the world's greatest kids from Columbine, Harrington, Graland, Slavens, and Frostwood Elementary Schools. These students were a joy to work with, and we treasure every minute spent with them. The real beginnings of *The Primary Toolkit* go back to the many teachers and kids we have worked with over the years. It is their best thinking that we have tried to capture and re-create here.

This work rests on the shoulders of many extraordinary educators, and we thank them all. A special thanks to David Pearson, whose thinking permeates the *Toolkit*. His insight, brilliance, humor, and commitment challenge us all to keep thinking and learning. And many thanks to David Perkins, professor, researcher, and out-of-the-box thinker, from whom we derived our notion of Active Literacy. Thanks, too, to Donald Graves, who connected us to *first*hand and believed in this project from the start, for his life's work in support of teachers and kids.

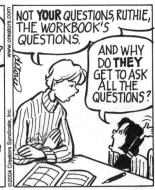

Reprinted by permission of Rick Detorie and Creator's Syndicate, Inc.

The Primary Comprehension Toolkit

Quick Start Guide

Young children are passionate about the real world. Nonfiction offers the most direct route to exploring it. For many K–2 kids, informational text is the gateway to engaged literacy. *The Primary Comprehension Toolkit* contains 22 strategy lessons, a variety of text and posters for teaching them, three classroom videos of comprehension instruction in action, additional resources for teaching and learning, and a *Teacher's Guide* to explain it all.

The Primary Toolkit comprehension curriculum easily integrates with your

- ➤ Reader's Workshop
- ➤ Balanced Literacy program
- ➤ Basal program
- ➤ Science and Social Studies curriculum

Getting Started with the *Toolkit*

IF YOU *want to see primary comprehension **instruction in action:***
Watch the Harvey and Goudvis classroom videos on the DVD

IF YOU *want to see what **Active Literacy Classrooms** look like:*
View the "Active Literacy Slideshow" on the DVD and read pages 20–28 in the *Teacher's Guide*

IF YOU *want to know how* Toolkit *teaching fits into your **reading program and schedule:***
Read pages 29–32 and 50–55 in the *Teacher's Guide*

IF YOU *want to see how* Toolkit *teaching works in **Science and Social Studies:***
Watch the "Reading, Writing, and Research in Science and Social Studies" slideshow on the DVD, view the "Content Literacy" video with Brad Buhrow, and read pages 59–64 in the *Teacher's Guide*

IF YOU *wonder how we **assess kids' growth** in reading and understanding:*
Page through any of the six strategy books and examine the "Reflect and Assess" sections near the end of each lesson, and read the *Teacher's Guide*, pages 56–58

IF YOU *want to **review the research** that validates comprehension instruction and nonfiction literacy:*
Read pages 65–68 in the *Teacher's Guide* and see the research articles on the DVD

IF YOU *want a **full picture** of* Toolkit *philosophy, practices, and procedures:*
Go to the *Teacher's Guide* and review sections accordingly

IF YOU *want to see the **wide array of student text** in the* Toolkit:
See *Keep Reading! A Source Book of Short Text*

IF YOU *are ready to **launch the lessons** with your class:*
Begin with *Strategy Book 1, Monitoring Comprehension*

HEINEMANN

Contents

Welcome to the *Toolkit*

Teaching with the *Toolkit*

Welcome to the *Toolkit*

"Teaching the young ones to read is such a treat.
This is the age of wonder, energy, curiosity, silliness, and enthusiasm."
Stephanie Harvey & Anne Goudvis

Thinking about
Young Readers

Primary teachers have the most important job in all of education—welcoming young children to the amazing world of reading. Helping kids to understand, enjoy, remember, and apply what they read is the most important single gift a teacher can ever give. Learning to read carefully and deeply opens doors that can never be slammed shut. Reading is the gateway to a boundless world of information, amazement, amusement, and problem-solving.

But here's our little secret: teaching the young ones to read is such a treat! This is the age of wonder, energy, curiosity, silliness, and enthusiasm. K–2 teachers have a unique privilege and responsibility: to get kids off to a strong start with literacy and with school. And we see progress—big-time. We get to savor the learning, the powerful strides, the measurable growth, from month to month, and on through the year. The kids change and grow before our eyes.

And the children in our classrooms are so deliciously different from each other. Between kindergarten and second grade is the biggest developmental span in all of schooling. Some kindergarteners come to us never having read a book or even a sentence, and perhaps unable to write their own names. Meanwhile, other kids are burning through books at school and at home, writing and illustrating their own stories, poems, and informational text. What a range!

But even the youngest of our students can "read" the red octagon that is a stop sign. Regardless of the formal literacy opportunities kids may have had at home, all primary kids come to us with a vast, lifelong experience of "reading the world," making sense of what they see, hear, and experience around them. As Regie Routman says, "every child enters the world comprehending, from the moment of their birth" (2007). Indeed, each of our primary students is a veteran comprehender. And it is precisely this emerging thinking that we build upon in our classrooms—and in *The Primary Comprehension Toolkit (PTK)*.

In *PTK* we keep reading simple, focused, and fun. This resource is designed to help K–2 kids understand what they view, hear, and read. For us, the most important goal of all—for grownups or kindergarteners—is to make sense of those marks on the page, to construct meaning by merging the author's words with our own thinking. Research has conclusively shown that skillful readers employ a repertoire of specific cognitive strategies to unlock meaning and provide understanding (Pearson and Duke, 2002). We want to teach these strategies to kids as early as possible, from kindergarten right on up.

And the little ones can handle it. Children are eager to find out what's in the world and how it works. Kids are ready to work hard, not because we "motivate" them, but because *they want to know stuff*. As teachers we can draw on all the curiosity, energy, and comprehending experience that kids bring to school, and we systematically link to the skills and strategies that more experienced learners use. People too often underestimate what primary kids can do. But in *The Primary Comprehension Toolkit*, we *start high and go higher*.

Origins of the Program

This new resource grew out of the original *The Comprehension Toolkit* for grades 3–6, which we developed and published in 2005. Since then, we have visited many classrooms around the country where the *Toolkit* has been implemented with intermediate-grade kids. Everywhere we traveled, teachers and district leaders asked us (increasingly loudly) to create a primary version of the *Toolkit*. They wanted a reading comprehension curriculum that could work seamlessly right up through the grades in an elementary building.

So we took the hint, and what a labor of love creating the primary edition has been! Over the past couple of years, we have visited and worked in scores of primary class-rooms, learning with kids and teachers in wonderful kindergarten, first-, and second-grade rooms from Boulder to Birmingham to Boston. Out of these intensive years of development and our own innumerable years in elementary classrooms (don't ask!), we developed the twenty-two lessons that are the core of this new *Primary Comprehension Toolkit* for K–2.

The Primary Comprehension Toolkit is not an add-on or an extra. The *Toolkit* replaces fill-in-the-blank activities and worksheets with engaging practices that foster active thinking and literacy. It helps students negotiate informational text, think about what they are reading, and hold that thinking so that they understand and remember it—and can use it to guide new learning.

The *Toolkit* provides explicit instruction. It uses techniques of modeling, practice, and application to promote diverse, flexible thinking. It encourages young kids to extend their learning beyond the text at hand, to ask questions that will lead to new learning. With *PTK*, we are able to create intellectually charged primary-grade classrooms that invite deep thinking and welcome questions, discussion, and debate.

Why Nonfiction?

With all the concern *that* kids read, we often forget the importance of *what* they read.

In conventional schooling, we have relied almost exclusively upon fiction—stories, fairy tales, folk tales, etc.—to introduce literacy to young ones. And there's nothing wrong with that magical body of literature as a foundation for kids' early literacy experience. Indeed, some of the *Toolkit* lessons and the *Toolkit* Trade Book Pack include stories, narrative text, and even delectable poetry.

But fiction doesn't necessarily entice everyone—and nonfiction can be a different, equally powerful *way in* to reading, especially for little kids. Listen as they gasp when you reveal the cover of a book about spiders, sharks, or dinosaurs. Hear their

"wows" when they learn about tornadoes, tidal waves, and coral reefs. Questions bubble right out of them when their curiosity is activated: "How does that work? How many? When? Why? What if?" When kids encounter fascinating topics, amazing information, and dramatic photos, they want to know more. They talk with friends and, over time, create their own writing, drawings, posters, and books. And there's no better genre than nonfiction to spur thinking in our developing readers. After all, they can get information from nonfiction without even having to read the words. Photos, illustrations, maps, and the like convey stimulating content and compelling information all on their own. There is nothing like a large *National Geographic* coffee table book opened to a two-page spread of a solar system map to get even the youngest kids thinking and wondering about space!

You get the picture. As much as we love and read fiction ourselves, we worry that nonfiction is underrepresented in schools. And this imbalance persists despite the fact that so many kids love nonfiction, grown-ups buy it, life requires it, and standardized tests include it even more than fiction in their high-stakes questions. So in the *Toolkit*, the majority of our lessons and materials focus on that broad range of fascinating "true" material called *informational* or *nonfiction* text.

In the *Toolkit* we have expanded our notion of nonfiction to include any form or genre from which we learn information. The *Toolkit* offers magazines, feature articles, large posters, realistic fiction picture books, poetry, and nonfiction trade books to expand kids' appetites for investigating the real world through reading.

Getting Started with Nonfiction

As we get ready to teach the *Toolkit* lessons, we set up our classrooms for nonfiction instruction and we help our kids understand the characteristics of nonfiction. We want them to understand the nature of nonfiction and differentiate it from other genres. Here are some suggestions for setting the stage for nonfiction literacy instruction.

- Flood the room with nonfiction on the widest range of topics and levels—trade books, picture books, big books, wordless books, short nonfiction guided-reading books, posters, magazines, newspapers, and the like. Don't forget to talk with your school librarian, who is likely the best resource for texts and topics. Also head to your public library, where they will generally lend scads of books to public schools for several weeks at a time. And don't ignore online resources, which continue to grow by leaps and bounds every year. To that end, check out the list of books, magazines, and web sites for short text and interesting topics in the bibliography in *Keep Reading! A Source Book of Short Text.*

- Fill the room with accessible tools and resources—markers, pencils, Post-its in a variety of sizes, drawing paper, differentiated writing paper, construction paper, scissors, glue, etc. Arrange them in baskets at students' tables and in convenient locations around the room so kids can get to them easily.

- Subscribe to magazines such as *National Geographic Young Explorer, Time For Kids (TFK), Scholastic News, Click, Appleseeds,* and *Ask.* If money is tight, you don't need a subscription for each classroom. A couple of school-wide subscriptions can go a long way to support our kids as they read, write, and think about information. The *TFK* posters and magazines and the *National Geographic Young Explorer* magazine included in the *Toolkit* can give you a taste of what is available.

- Don't miss opportunities to find and save large-format texts. They promote visual literacy and give young learners a great chance to think and wonder about the images as well as the text. You simply can't have too many big books or posters for primary kids for both modeling and shared reading. Think of ways to find materials for little cost or even for free. Old photographic calendars are a gold mine! World Wildlife Fund calendars are among the best. People just throw them away, so get the word out that you want them. Bookstores often sell calendars for half price in early January. Posters abound at fast-food restaurants, which are usually happy to save them for a passionate teacher! Think creatively to scare up resources.

- Place books in baskets in accessible locations around the room. Label them by topic—animals, space, cultures, Antarctica, ecology, etc.

- Place some texts in baskets by author, as some authors are particularly known for their nonfiction writing: Gail Gibbons, Helen Cowcher, Joanna Cole, Louise Borden, Ann Rockwell, Seymour Simon, Stephen Kramer, Donald Crews, Tomie dePaola, Kathryn Lasky, and Andrea Davis Pinkney, to name a few—or any other nonfiction writers that you love.

- Model how to skim and scan a nonfiction text, looking at the cover, photos, illustrations, and bold print to get an idea of what the book is about and determine our interest in it.

- Hold what our friend and colleague Kathy Leerson calls "a book frenzy." Children sit in a circle with nonfiction texts in their hands. Give them each about 30 seconds or so to soak up the text—skimming and scanning—before you announce that it's time to hand it over to the next child and try a new one. Continue this for 15 minutes or so. Most kids will emerge as committed nonfiction readers who can't wait to get their hands on the book that really grabbed them!

- Encourage kids to pore over nonfiction materials individually, in pairs, or in small groups. Get them to notice how these texts look different from the stories they have read. Have kids talk about and record what they notice about the text and about nonfiction in general.

- Show how you review the books in your nonfiction collection, classifying them by topic, author, or informational genre. Model the difference between books that are science related and those that are social studies related. This is a great way to get young kids to think about the difference between these two content areas. And remember to explain that sometimes a topic in a book may be both scientific and cultural. For example, books about the rain forest might have scientific information about deforestation and the destruction of animal habitat, but also include cultural information about the lifestyles of the people who live in the rain forest.

- Model the differences between fiction and nonfiction and some truths about each genre.

  - Nonfiction is true and real. Fiction is made up but can seem real.

  - The term *nonfiction* is confusing for young kids. They get thrown off by the *non*. They often think it means *not real*, so clarify this from the get-go.

  - Show how to check out the cover to get an idea of whether a text is fiction or nonfiction.

  - Show nonfiction books and explain that they give us true information. We can usually tell by the cover what a nonfiction text is going to teach us, whereas the cover of a fiction book does not always reveal explicitly what it is about.

  - When there are photographs rather than drawings, the text is usually nonfiction.

  - When the animals are talking, it is almost certainly fiction!

  - Pay attention to the photographs and illustrations in the text. Visuals are of great importance in nonfiction, and we want kids to include art when they write nonfiction—creating posters, picture books, etc.

- Note the many different features sprinkled throughout nonfiction texts: graphs, charts, maps, etc. (Nonfiction features are explained in depth in several lessons in Strategy Book 1.)

- Model, use, and make sure kids understand vocabulary that is particularly useful when investigating nonfiction: *true, accurate, real, information, photo, image, research*, etc. These terms are explored in further depth in the *Toolkit* lessons.

- Co-construct an Anchor Chart entitled *Characteristics of Nonfiction*. Record what kids have learned about nonfiction as well as anything else you believe should be on the chart.

- Co-construct a large Venn diagram with the headings *Nonfiction, Both, Fiction*. Have kids think about not only how nonfiction and fiction are different, but also how they are similar.

  Some differences: Nonfiction has real information. Fiction is made up. Fiction has characters. Nonfiction does not, etc.

  Some similarities: Both have titles on the cover, both have illustrations, both have authors who have written them, etc.

Nonfiction Features
that Give Information and Signal Importance

Text Features

Fonts and Effects   Text features are those nonfiction features that are created with words and symbols. Teachers can share examples and explicitly teach different fonts and effects, such as titles, headings, subheads, captions, labels, framed text, bold print, color print, italics, bullets, and so on. We can remind kids that font and effect differences should be viewed as signal flags that say, "This is important. Pay attention."

Text Organizers   Teachers can teach about how texts are organized by sharing examples such as indexes, glossaries, tables of contents, chapter headings, and appendices. When kids are looking through texts for information, understanding the purpose of these text organizers is very helpful.

Visual Features

Illustrations and Photographs   Visual literacy is key. Illustrations play a prominent role in nonfiction learning. The most common visual features are illustrations and photographs. Nonfiction trade books and magazines brim with colorful visual features that kidnap young readers and carry them deeper into meaning.

Graphics   More elaborate and specific visual features include diagrams, cut-aways, cross-sections, overlays, maps, distribution maps, word bubbles, tables, graphs, and charts. These visual features inform nonfiction readers of important information.

What Is Comprehension and How Do We Teach It?

Too often in primary grades, we have defined comprehension as the ability to answer factual recall questions ("What color was the kitten?") or to retell a story. While both of these kinds of thinking are valuable (and perhaps even foundational) they do not tell anywhere near the whole story of comprehension.

Reading comprehension is the evolution of thought that occurs as we read. True understanding happens when readers merge their thinking with the text, ask questions, draw inferences, think about what's important, and summarize and synthesize. This enables them to use their new understanding to ask further questions and guide new learning. This active, constructive, strategic thinking process entails far more than simply retelling.

Unfortunately, this well-documented view of comprehension hasn't been universally understood or implemented. Instead, many schools still follow the tradition of breaking reading down into its component behaviors, teaching these "subskills" separately with hope that kids will later put it all together, some day.

But reading is not just behaviors, it is thinking. And reading is always about meaning. Anytime we try to split off subskills of reading for very long, we cut kids off from the purpose of reading itself. In the old days, schools used to instruct kids in phonics first, and move on to meaning and comprehension later (sometimes years later). What were we thinking? That approach sometimes had kindergarteners, first-, and even second-graders spending huge chunks of time doing isolated-skill worksheets before they were allowed to read real text.

We now understand that children need what David Perkins (2008, in press) calls "whole game" learning. In whole game learning, kids orchestrate all the same elements that "real players" (i.e. adults) use in the "game of thinking." While it may be OK to practice free-throws in your driveway for a while, your basketball skills only come to fruition in a real game where you have to put it all together in a whole complex context. Same for reading. There's nothing wrong with splitting out certain skills and practicing them apart from whole text experiences. But we always have to be playing the whole reading "game," where kids encounter authentic text, *and* where making meaning, not practicing subskills, is the central activity.

Today we understand that we must teach all elements of reading at once so that kids constantly practice what proficient readers do: put it all together. We don't confine literacy learning to the reading/writing block in the daily schedule. We extend reading, thinking, and learning across the whole school day.

Six Key Strategies

Our primary grade comprehension instruction centers on the specific kinds of thinking that proficient readers have been shown to use. We have extensively reviewed and explicated this research in our book, *Strategies That Work: Teaching Comprehension for Understanding and Engagement* (Second Edition, Stenhouse, 2007).

No matter what their age, effective readers use the following six strategies:

Monitor Comprehension

When readers monitor their comprehension, they keep track of their thinking as they read, listen, and view. They notice when the text makes sense and when it doesn't. They distinguish between what the text is about and what it makes them think about. Primary-grade kids are always thinking about what they hear, see, and (if they can) read. They are noticing, wondering, making connections, and making judgments all the time. When they monitor their comprehension, they use that awareness to steer their thinking as they enter texts. They expect to interact with the pictures, the features, the words, and the ideas. Rather than simply retelling the story, kids need to go beyond retelling to merge their thinking with the text. This is how they come up with the "big ideas." So we focus on teaching kids not just to retell, but to think about the words, the pictures, the features, and the ideas that spring from the text. They stay on track when they talk, draw, and write about their thinking. By interacting with the text and with each other, they gain understanding.

Activate and Connect

David Pearson reminds us that "Today's new knowledge is tomorrow's background knowledge" (2006). The background knowledge we bring to learning colors every aspect of our understanding. Whether we are connecting, questioning, or inferring, background knowledge is the foundation of our thinking. We simply can't understand what we hear, read, or view without thinking about what we already know. To comprehend, learners must connect the new to the known. So we consider every conceivable way to build our kids' background knowledge to prepare them to learn new information. We begin by encouraging young learners to think about what they already know and care about, and then have them explore those topics. As kids go on to read widely in nonfiction, they are bombarded with new information. In order to understand it, they need to merge their thinking with the information, stopping and reacting as they go. By making connections to what they already know, they make sense of their new learning and acquire new knowledge.

Ask Questions

Curiosity is at the heart of teaching and learning. Young kids burst through the door bubbling over with questions: "Why is the sky blue? Where does the sun go at night? What happened to the cowboys?" Questions spur curious minds to investigate. Questions open doors to understanding the world. We have to mine them with a pickax! When young readers read nonfiction and meet new information, they brim with questions. As we try to answer our questions, we discover new information and gain knowledge. Questions can spur further research and inquiry. Instead of demanding answers all the time, we need to teach kids to ask thoughtful and insightful questions. After all, if we hope to develop critical thinkers, we must teach our kids to think about and question what they listen to, read, and view. Asking questions enriches the learning experience and leads to deeper understanding. Questioning is the strategy that propels learners forward.

Infer and Visualize

Inferring is the bedrock of understanding. It involves taking what you know, your background knowledge, and merging it with clues in the text to come up with some information that isn't explicitly stated. Inferential thinking helps readers to figure out unfamiliar words, draw conclusions, develop interpretations, make predictions, surface themes, and even create mental images.

Visualizing is sort of a first cousin to inferring. When readers visualize, they construct meaning by creating mental images, seeing, hearing, tasting, touching, and even smelling! Young children seem particularly inclined to visualize in support of understanding as they listen to and read stories, often living through or living in the stories. When children infer and visualize as they listen, read, and view, they respond with joy, glee, or sometimes dread. Inferring and visualizing enable kids to get at the deeper meaning in text.

Determine Importance

When we read nonfiction, we are reading to learn and remember information. Once kids know how to merge their thinking with the information, it's time to help them figure out what makes sense to remember. We can't possibly remember every fact or piece of information we read, nor should we. We teach kids to tell the difference between interesting details and salient, important information. When kids learn to paraphrase, they are well on their way to understanding the information and shaping it into their own thought. In *PTK*, kids also learn to distinguish between facts, questions, and responses so they can sort and sift information to better organize it. They use note-taking scaffolds to hold their thinking as they prepare to share it with others.

Summarize and Synthesize

Synthesizing information nudges kids to see the "big picture." It pulls together their thinking, and they learn as they read and write about it. It's not enough for readers to simply recall or restate the facts. They need to use a variety of comprehension strategies including asking questions, inferring, and determining what's important, to understand big ideas. We begin by simply asking young readers to stop and collect their thoughts before reading on. Eventually, children summarize and synthesize their thinking by drawing and writing in all sorts of original ways: creating poems, posters, books, and other projects that demonstrate their learning and understanding. Most importantly, synthesizing has an authentic purpose: kids share their learning with their peers and teachers, who respond with their thoughts and ideas. In this way, the classroom becomes a community of learners in which everyone is both a learner and a teacher.

Toolkit
Comprehension Instruction

For the K–2 *Toolkit*, we have developed twenty-two lessons around these key thinking strategies—three or four lessons for each. Every lesson is designed to introduce, reinforce, and extend one of the strategies to enhance understanding. It begins with one of us modeling the lesson with a specific text, taking kids through all the steps of reading, writing, talking, and thinking. Then it offers a template—the Lesson Guide—that you may use to design your own instruction, using any text you choose.

People sometimes wonder, "Can five-, six-, and seven-year-olds really think like this? Can they truly infer, synthesize, and all the rest?" You bet! Notice what happens when you read a great book aloud to your kids, gathered on the rug. You realize that they are **monitoring their comprehension** when they raise their hands to **ask questions** about the text or to clarify misunderstandings about the information. You know that children are **connecting** when they blurt out comments like "I know a butterfly sucks nectar—I saw one do it!" You understand that kids are **visualizing**, because if you ask them to imagine a whale breeching, they'll offer detailed and different descriptions. You know that they are **inferring** when they can merge their own experience with the text to respond thoughtfully to the language in a poem, or to realize that something scary is about to happen. You realize that kids are **determining importance** because they are able to understand why we remember a famous person. And you know that children are **summarizing and synthesizing** because most of them can discuss why the rain forests of the world are in danger— or speculate about why the author wrote the book.

The Primary Comprehension Toolkit emphasizes responsive teaching. We continually watch, listen, keep track of, and document our students' learning, stepping in with additional support as we determine it's needed, pulling back and letting kids take the lead when they show us they know how. And we respond to our students' needs and challenges as they reveal—through our assessment data—what's working for them and what's not.

Principles that
Guide Our Work

In an Active Literacy Classroom, all members of the classroom community work collaboratively. Teachers and students alike view themselves as thinkers, learners, and teachers. Our teaching within *The Primary Comprehension Toolkit* is shaped by twelve guiding principles.

Teach for Understanding and Engagement

Kids' thinking matters! When our students begin to understand that their thinking matters, reading changes. The refrain of "What time is recess? When is lunch?" becomes an anthem of "Can we please go read now?" As teachers, we take kids' thoughts, ideas, and opinions seriously. We design instruction that engages kids and guides them as they grapple with the information and concepts they encounter in school. We teach the reader, not merely the reading, modeling thinking strategies that allow our kids to construct meaning. We teach them to activate and connect to background knowledge, ask and answer questions, infer and visualize meaning, determine what's important, and summarize and synthesize learning. To understand and engage in what they are learning, kids interact with the text, with each other, and with their teachers.

Create an Environment for Active Literacy

We build in time every day for kids to read, write, draw, talk, listen, and investigate. Inside a classroom that values active literacy, room arrangement is thoughtful and fosters social interaction. Work spaces encourage collaboration. We provide areas around the room that encourage student-to-student and teacher-to-student interaction. We co-construct meaning in large groups, small groups, conferences, and through discussions where everyone gets a chance to weigh in. Our schedule allows time for purposeful student-to-student talk throughout the day. After the collaborative and independent practice time concludes, kids have opportunities to share with the whole group.

Understand that Text Matters

> *It is not enough to simply teach children to read: we have to give them something worth reading. Something that will stretch their imagination—something that will help them make sense of their own lives and encourage them to reach out toward people whose lives are quite different from their own.*
> *Katherine Paterson (1995)*

As Katherine Paterson reminds us, text matters! A lot. If kids are not reading or listening to engaging, interesting, thought-provoking text, why bother? We need to provide opportunities to read text worth thinking about. Students need a steady diet of texts that present a variety of perspectives and a broad range of content topics. When students read texts that raise significant issues and provoke thinking, they become active readers. Young children need not be protected from important or complex topics. They aren't afraid of big ideas. If we feed them books about apples, they'll study apples. But if we feed them books about justice, they'll read and think and write and talk and draw about justice.

And choice matters, too! Kids should read text they can and want to read. They should read about what matters to them and find out things they didn't know before. In order to focus on content, topics, and issues, we use a multisource, multigenre, multimedia curriculum. We're not reticent to say it: half of our success as teachers is getting the right books into the kids' hands! For little ones especially, the right book can ignite them, launching them into a lifetime of reading.

Foster Passion and Curiosity

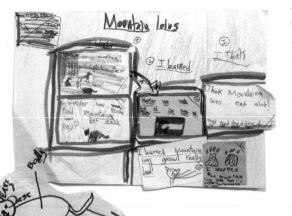

Passion and wonder are central to life in an Active Literacy Classroom. Students enter our classrooms brimming with curiosity about the world and are encouraged to ask questions and explore a range of texts and resources to find answers. Projects that require students to actively use, evaluate, and synthesize information are much more likely to engage kids. That's why, when we walk into a room where the focus is on reading nonfiction, we know it right away. Nonfiction reading can be messy and noisy. The classroom echoes with the "ooohs," "ahhhs," and "oh-my-goshes" that may come from viewing a photograph of a swirling tornado or a flock of toucans flying over the rain forest canopy. We need to give kids time to read nonfiction independently, but we also need to recognize that they may not be able to stop themselves from shaking the shoulder of the kid next to them with "Whoa, take a look at the wingspan of this pterodactyl!" That's what happens when we nurture kids' passion and wonder.

Share Our Literate Lives

Teachers can set the standard by being thoughtful readers and learners themselves. As the custodians of the teaching of reading, we teachers must be prolific readers. We must read to nurture the soul and gain information as well as to understand our own reading process. Our kids must know we are readers. We can let them know this by modeling effective comprehension strategies with our own reading. And we can talk to kids about what we are reading. We share how we read the newspaper every Sunday and how we look through poetry to give our friends poems on their birthdays. We bring in a novel that we are reading in our neighborhood book club and model how we clear up confusion by asking a question. We show how we read movie reviews online. We can share our passion and love of reading daily so our students make no mistake about the fact that we are readers. Every day we can let kids know how reading changes and enriches our lives.

Create a Common Language for Literacy and Learning

When students use a common language across the grade levels and the curriculum, they can better understand, learn from one another, and process information. So we teach the language of comprehension and strategic thinking because we want kids to adopt and adapt our teaching language as their learning language. Kids learn what it means to infer, to synthesize, or to connect to background knowledge, and they use this common language to express their thinking. Now, sometimes when people hear five- and six-year-olds fluently talking about inferences or text-to-world connections, they wonder: "Is this for real?" And when they see kids conducting their own sharing circles using polite language ("Thank you, Abdul. Does anyone else have any questions, comments, or connections?"), they may ask: "Are these kids just parroting this language, or do they really understand what they are saying?" In our lessons, we teach kids a lot of highly conceptual ideas and the language that goes with them. And we look for evidence of their understanding through their work and their words.

Build Instruction Around Real-World Reading

Consider your daily reading material. Chances are you're like most adults and much of your reading life centers on short nonfiction: newspapers, magazine articles, memos, directions, essays, editorials, and so on. Often in school, students engage in focused content reading and have little opportunity for real-world reading. *Both are essential.* When kids read "widely and wildly," as Shelley Harwayne (2000) recommends, they are far more likely to find content that intrigues them and that propels them to investigate further. This kind of reading also helps build

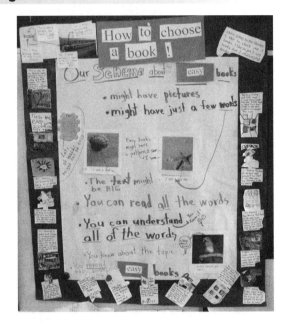

background across a wide range of topics, both familiar and unfamiliar. In this way, kids develop a reservoir of knowledge from which they can draw to understand future texts.

Provide Explicit Instruction with the Gradual Release of Responsibility Framework

We provide explicit instruction through the Gradual Release of Responsibility framework: modeling, guided practice, collaborative practice, and independent practice. Showing our thinking and modeling the mental processes we go through when we read give students an idea of what thoughtful readers do. In this way, we make our thinking visible for all of our kids. We explicitly teach reading comprehension strategies by demonstrating them for students in large groups, small groups, and conferences. We guide kids as they practice together and on their own so they become independent learners who take initiative. Gradual Release applies to choice of text as well as instruction. We begin with text that supports readers to understand what we are teaching and give them opportunities to tackle more challenging text later on.

Make Thinking Visible

To make thinking visible, we record, draw, chart, and talk about our learning. Throughout the day, teachers model their thinking to make their own learning process visible so that students can understand how learning happens. Students leave tracks of their thinking through writing and drawing, so they can take it public, sharing it with their peers for further discussion.

Co-constructed Anchor Charts provide a place for the whole class to record their thinking and learning and hold it for later consideration. Sharing thinking in large groups, small groups, or in pairs provides a chance for children to hear the perspectives, thoughts, and concerns of others. When students make their thinking visible, engaging in substantive conversations and writing and drawing in response to reading, they are better able to articulate and understand their learning.

Recognize that Reading, Writing, and Art Are Interconnected and Synergistic

Kids don't learn to read and then sometime later learn to write. Drawing and writing are crucial ways of exploring and learning about print. Drawing is often the most effective way for young kids to demonstrate their learning and understanding. Indeed, creating their own texts, through a mix of drawing and writing, is a key pathway to literacy. From playing with scribble writing, to employing increasingly accurate invented spellings, and onward to conventional writing, many children come to reading through drawing and writing. And, of course, the process is reciprocal: as kids draw and write their way into reading, their growing reading lives enrich and inform their drawing and writing. Kids' art-making is much more than a charming decoration for refrigerator doors at home—it is a representational activity vital to their development as readers, writers, and thinkers.

Differentiate Instruction Paying Special Attention to the Needs of Developing Readers and English Language Learners

One size does not fit all. We consider how our instruction, materials, and assessments can be adapted to students with varying reading proficiencies, learning styles, and language backgrounds. Instruction occurs in a variety of groupings—large groups, small groups, pairs, and with individuals. These methods of differentiation make sense for all kids. But we keep a special eye out for our English Language Learners and adjust our speaking, listening, and comprehending challenges accordingly. And, of course, when appropriate, we provide our ELL kids with great text in their home language so they can gain information and build background information more easily.

Teach with the End in Mind

By looking carefully and listening to our kids' words and thoughts, we derive an authentic understanding of what they are doing and what they have learned or not learned. When we reflect on the evidence of children's learning and understanding, we revise and shape our subsequent instruction. This is what we call the *teaching-assessing loop*. Authentic assessment informs us about three things: children's learning and understanding, the effectiveness of our past instruction, and where we need to go next. Responsive teaching and assessment go hand in hand. We use evidence of what we see in students' work to tailor future instruction to their needs. Conferring with students is the best way we know to assess their learning needs. We listen carefully to students' responses in conversation and review their drawings, jots on Post-its, and writing of any sort.

How to Create an
Active Literacy Classroom

Reading, writing, drawing, talking, listening, and investigating are the cornerstones of active literacy. *The Primary Comprehension Toolkit* is all about active learning and responsive teaching. The end result is a lively classroom where our youngest kids are engaged in diverse thinking, spirited discussion, and deep understanding.

An Active Literacy Classroom fairly bursts with joyful, enthusiastic learning. Throughout the day, kids are actively questioning, discussing, debating, reading, drawing, writing, investigating, extending their learning, and generating new questions. We can't read kids' minds, but one way to open a window into their understanding is to help them surface, talk, draw, and write about their thinking. Active literacy is the means to deeper understanding and diverse, flexible thinking, and is the hallmark of our approach to teaching and learning. The *Toolkit* captures the language of thinking we use to explicitly teach kids to comprehend the wide variety of informational text they encounter.

To create an Active Literacy Classroom that hums with productive learning shaped by our guiding principles, we rely on the following instructional practices that provide structure and support learning.

To see comprehension instruction in an Active Literacy Classroom, watch the "Active Literacy Slideshow" and the "Three Classroom Videos" on *The Primary Comprehension Toolkit DVD-ROM*.

The way the room is set up—the way books are arranged, supplies are provided, and how we use different spaces—all these make a crucial difference in the way kids learn. We create an environment that inspires kids to think, imagine, and act.

Room Arrangement

When we set up a literate environment, we put a lot of thought into room arrangement. For whole-class instruction, we create a large, comfortable meeting space on the floor. When we provide instruction, we need kids up close and personal so they can focus on our teaching and their learning. We also create comfortable meeting places where small groups of kids can sit up close as we model instruction. Desks in clusters or tables where they can practice and work are scattered throughout. We create large spaces on the floor for kids to spread out and work together or alone and quiet places where kids can work independently.

Books and Classroom Libraries

Primary kids need tons of books—rich, varied, intriguing books—and magazines, pictures, reference volumes, articles, posters, and more. The better and bigger our classroom libraries get, the more choices we will have in planning lessons, hooking kids, and feeding genuine inquiry. Of course, developing a classroom library is the work of months and years, not just one initial order! You might even say it is a labor of love that unfolds over a career. Yes, we can and do teach well from a modest supply of books—but for truly great instruction, we need to grow the range of titles as quickly and smartly as we can. Don't forget to head to the school library and check with your librarian for the latest, most captivating titles for your kids.

Book Organization

When books are organized in a logical and inviting way, kids can easily find the ones they want to read. For primary grades, one of the most accessible arrangements is to have assorted baskets of books right on top of work tables, so kids can reach out and grab a great book without even having to get out of their chairs. We are careful to include a variety of books on different levels. And we teachers needn't prearrange everything ourselves—kids love to organize the books in their classroom, categorizing them by genre, topic, and author.

Materials and Resources

Materials and resources that are easily accessible promote independent work. Clipboards act as portable desks so kids can interact with us, with each other, and with the text. Tools are readily available—markers, pencils, glue, and other supplies are kept in multiple places to foster kids' independence. We create a culture of abundance, not scarcity, so kids' expression is never delayed by a hunt for materials.

Post-its

Post-its are a tool for kids to quickly capture and hold their thinking. The small size seems to be liberating; indeed, where kids may just write a few words or lines in a notebook, they easily cover multiple Post-its. We encourage children to use jumbo Post-its for their drawing and art and smaller ones for their writing. We also use Post-its to scribe what kids say when they cannot yet write on their own. And we often have kids think through ways to organize multiple Post-its to summarize and synthesize their learning! For an alternative to expensive Post-its, use our Post-it templates found among the print resources in the back of each Strategy Book and on the DVD-ROM. There are two templates for your convenience: one with six 3″ × 3″ squares and one with three 3″ × 5″ spaces.

Halls and Walls

In classrooms that promote active literacy, halls and walls teach. They burst with examples of kids' thinking and understanding. They showcase student writing, drawing, and art—so everyone can learn from it. Children love working big and are excited to share what they have learned on large charts and posters. Rather than filling the walls with commercial posters at the start of the school year, teachers leave plenty of space for kids' emerging work, which gradually creates "learning walls" instead of mere decorations.

Promote Engaged Thinking and Learning

Passion and wonder are contagious. We've never found a kid we can't hook on something in the real world. When we provide kids with great text and opportunities to talk about it, children are going to learn and have fun along the way.

Text Matters

Yes, we are repeating ourselves—on purpose. Kids need books they *can* read and *want to* read, every single day. The quality and breadth of text (and visuals) that we offer young readers is more important than any particular lesson we could ever plan. Building a classroom library of great text is something we work at year in and year out, adding new selections that excite our kids' curiosity and wonder.

Reading for Information

In classrooms that promote active literacy, children read a wide range of genres, topics, formats, and authors. Nonfiction rises to the surface in the primary grades because of its accessibility—even the youngest kids can "read" the photographs, illustrations, and other text features. Reading a wide variety of nonfiction text on diverse topics builds kids' background knowledge. Kids read signs, posters, wordless books, picture books, magazines, web articles, and more.

Strategic Thinking and Reading

The central focus of instruction in *The Primary Comprehension Toolkit* is on strategies that are particularly effective for helping readers think about and understand what they read, hear, or view. Kids learn to use strategies flexibly—monitoring comprehension, activating background knowledge, asking questions, drawing inferences, visualizing, determining importance, and summarizing and synthesizing. The strategies create a common language for understanding and discussing what we think. Kids demonstrate how they use strategies by reading, drawing, writing, and talking to each other.

Differentiated Instruction

In primary classrooms, kids invariably come to us at different stages of literacy development. One-on-one conferences are an especially powerful way to carefully target instruction to each child. We make information as concrete as possible, using photographs, drawings, charts, overheads, maps, and the like. Such visual aids help make concepts and ideas clear, providing English Language Learners multiple entry points into English instruction. And just as we differentiate our instruction, we vary our text, too. It's essential to offer readings on a wide range of topics.

Teach with the Gradual Release of Responsibility Framework

Research and common sense both tell us we cannot wait around hoping for kids to "catch on" to the ways that proficient readers think. We need to provide explicit instruction in reading-as-thinking every day.

The Gradual Release of Responsibility Model

In the Active Literacy Classroom, we frame instruction around the Gradual Release of Responsibility. When we provide instruction, primary kids need to get quickly engaged in doing the kind of thinking we have demonstrated or their attention is likely to flag. So we model our thinking briefly and then engage kids in the process, watching them right in front of us. Then we send kids out to practice collaboratively or independently. Gradual Release is not a linear process, but rather a recursive and dynamic one. We sometimes think of this rhythm as being quite like the "catch-and-release" cycle used by savvy fishermen: reel them in, toss them back for a swim, then reel them in again.

Read-Alouds

Jim Trelease, author of *The Read-Aloud Handbook* (2006), believes that "reading aloud serves to reassure, entertain, inform, explain, arouse curiosity, and inspire our kids." Although most teachers read fiction aloud on a regular basis, they sometimes forget the nonfiction. Reading nonfiction aloud is one of the best ways we know to build our kids' background knowledge. When teaching reading comprehension, we do a good deal of instruction via reading aloud. But we must remember that if we only read aloud for the purpose of instruction, we will ruin reading aloud. We need to read aloud every day for the sheer joy of it!

Interactive Read-Alouds

An interactive read-aloud is a shared reading practice to enhance comprehension. Interactive read-alouds are all about listening comprehension, which makes them an ideal instructional technique for young readers. In an interactive read-aloud, the teacher reads the text and guides the discussion while the students are bunched up on the floor with clipboards and pencils. They listen, talk to each other, and jot or draw their

The Gradual Release of Responsibility

Connect and Engage   Before we begin to model instruction, we capture our kids' enthusiasm and activate their background knowledge. We share a compelling image, an interesting title, or a personal story to get them excited about what's to come. And we have them turn and talk about their own experience and what they think they know about the topic at hand.

Modeling   As literacy teachers, we open up our own cognitive process to show kids how we read, sharing both our successes as readers and how we handle challenges along the way. We model instruction by thinking out loud, reading aloud interactively, and conducting shared readings.

Guided Practice   Much of our teaching and learning in the Active Literacy Classroom occurs during guided practice. We invite kids to turn and talk throughout the lesson so that they have a better shot at understanding. Guided practice allows us to respond to the kids while they practice up close to us and we scaffold our instruction to meet their needs.

Collaborative Practice   During collaborative practice, kids work in pairs or small groups to read, draw, write, and talk together as we move around the room conferring.

Independent Practice   The ultimate goal of instruction in the Active Literacy Classroom is to move kids toward independence. We want all kids to become confident, capable readers and thinkers who initiate further learning. So we allow plenty of classroom time for kids to practice the strategies on their own as we confer, assess, and coach them.

Sharing the Learning   As a community, we gather at all stages of our work to share what we are wondering and learning. Kids turn and talk during our minilessons, they talk together in small groups during collaborative practice, and they come back together in the end, teaching their classmates and responding to each others' ideas.

Adapted from Fielding and Pearson, 1994

thinking. With this practice, all kids are free to listen to and think about the ideas in the text because decoding doesn't interfere. They process the information by turning and talking throughout the instruction. Picture books, big books, posters, and charts offer great text for interactive read-alouds.

Think-Alouds

One of the key structures of the Gradual Release of Responsibility Framework is the "think-aloud" (Davey, 1983). In a think-aloud, we model our thinking for students. We open up our minds and show children how we actually think while reading. We peel back the layers of our thinking and show kids how we approach text and how understanding happens. To remove the cloak of mystery surrounding the comprehension process, we verbalize the thoughts we have as we read, surfacing the inner conversation we have with the text. This detailed process of making thinking public is a powerful way to make the reading-as-thinking concrete. Students come to view us as readers and observe our authentic reading process.

Encourage Social Interaction and Purposeful Talk

Literacy is a social act. In classrooms that promote active literacy, kids and teachers co-construct meaning, interacting with one another throughout the day. Everyone weighs in with their thinking. So in thinking classrooms we increase the amount of time that kids spend talking. This is not just idle conversation. We support kids' talk about important issues, ideas, concepts, and information. We understand that conversation deepens understanding.

Early in the year, we model a number of procedures that show kids how to engage in purposeful talk. We work to scaffold our collective conversation by providing opportunities for kids to talk in different settings, including partner, small-group, and large-group conversations. We model the structures by finding another adult or a willing student to be our partner. Whether it is turning and talking during a mini-lesson or sharing work with the whole class, we want all kids to understand what is expected of them during the lessons. We might ask a student to join us in front of the class so that others can watch the process in action. We read a little of the text out loud, and then students watch us turn and talk, share questions, explain what we learned, and comment on the information and ideas.

Here are some *Toolkit* structures for organizing kids' conversations.

Turn and Talk

Enter an Active Literacy Classroom, and you will see kids frequently turning and talking about their thinking. We simply must increase purposeful student-to-student talk in school, so that kids are active, engaged, and thinking all the time.

During whole-group instruction, frequently only the most vocal kids share their thinking. When providing whole-group instruction, we stop every few minutes to ask kids to turn to each other and share their thinking, giving them a better shot at understanding. We listen in as they talk to each other. After kids have had a moment to share with a partner, we ask several to share out with the group, particularly if we have heard something while they were partnered that we think the entire group should hear. Most of the kids, and particularly ELL students, are more articulate in front of the whole group when they have had a chance first to rehearse their thinking and talking with a partner.

Paired Reading

When we ask all kids to read the exact same text, it is quite possible that some students will not be able to due to the text difficulty. We often recommend that kids work with buddies or partners during collaborative practice. These partners change frequently so that kids get to know each other as readers. We make sure less-developed readers are partnered with readers proficient enough to read the text. It is not about pairing the most advanced readers with the least-developed ones; it is merely a strategy to ensure that no one will miss the text information because they are unable to read the text. When kids read in pairs, we stress the idea of *active listening*. We make it clear that the listener has the biggest job. The listener takes notes while listening to the reader—jotting or drawing any questions, connections, or reactions and then sharing those when the reader has finished reading.

Work Talk

When we turn kids loose to practice the strategies we have taught, we are happy to see them chatting in threes or fours or at tables. When we listen in, we usually find that what's happening is purposeful and supportive "work talk." Often kids will stop to marvel together at a picture in someone's book. Sometimes they will help each other with spelling a word. At other times, they will pause from their own thoughts and chew on someone's inquiry question. As they read, write, or draw, kids have the same kinds of conversations that co-workers or collaborators have when they sit side by side. These conversations enhance everyone's productivity.

Large-Group Shares

Whether we are gathered on the rug for an opening lesson, or gathered an hour later to share our thinking, whole-group discussion is a crucial social experience in the Active Literacy Classroom. When we meet as a community, we can share the widest possible range of responses. Whole-group sharing offers a terrific opportunity for kids to teach each other what they have learned. We value the distinctive contributions and the special voice of each and every person in the group.

When we come back to close the lesson, we often meet in a sharing circle. A circle is the perfect configuration for a culminating experience because kids' focus is on each other rather than the teacher.

Because discussion is the heartbeat of learning, we emphasize and demonstrate polite ways of talking with each other. Whole-group sharing sessions are not worth the time if no one is listening! Polite invitational sharing sets a tone that promotes listening and talking about the topic at hand. In fact, our teaching of these key social skills is integrated right into the lessons, so you'll see how we help kids develop the language of productive interaction. Their talk may seem stilted at first, but kids become accustomed to thanking each other and grow to appreciate that the polite stance encourages others to participate.

Throughout the day, kids have opportunities to share their thinking in many different settings—in large groups, small groups, and with partners. They draw, write, and talk about their thinking and learning. When kids take their thinking public by sharing it, they articulate their understanding and they learn from each other.

Kids' Drawing and Art

We must not underestimate the importance of art in primary classrooms. Drawing is perhaps the most effective way for young kids to demonstrate their learning and understanding. To make their thinking visible, kids jot and draw thinking on Post-its, thinksheets, in the margins, and on posters. They illustrate and add meaning to reports and projects with colorful and detailed artwork. As the year goes by, we often see kids' words carrying more and more meaning. But that doesn't mean the drawing doesn't matter anymore. None of us ever outgrows the usefulness of graphic strategies for pushing, shaping, and sharing thinking.

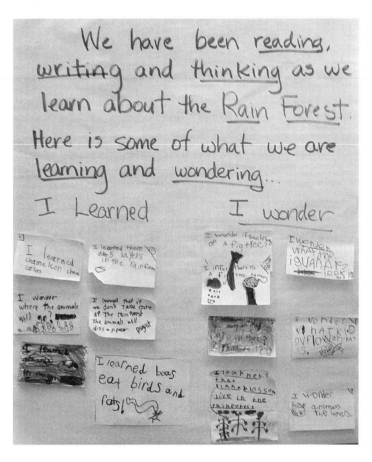

Anchor Charts

We construct Anchor Charts to record kids' thinking about a text, lesson, or strategy so that we can return to it later and remember the process. Kids play an important role in this process by adding their thinking through writing and drawing. The charts are a visual reminder of past instruction that we continue to build on. Anchor Charts connect past teaching and learning to future teaching and learning. They serve as reminders of what has come before so that we can better understand what is to come. Anchor Charts are not fixed and can be added to at any time.

Thinksheets: Scaffolds and Forms

We use a variety of scaffolds and forms, all of which include a place for kids to record their own responses and opinions. These include graphic organizers or what we like to call *thinksheets*. These may be double- and triple-column forms or response starters such as *I Learned/ I Wonder/Wow!* Annotating and jotting thinking in the margins of articles represents another form of thinksheet. Such note-taking or drawing scaffolds help readers understand and remember what they read. Unlike worksheets, which typically allow for just one right answer—and may only involve a yes/no, true/false answer, or multiple-choice format—thinksheets invite students to think deeply and widely about their own questions, opinions, reactions, and inferences.

Thinksheets promote engaged, active reading, help students sort out information, and encourage them to work out their thinking. As P. David Pearson reminds us, just as students show their work in mathematics, so we invite them to show their thinking about texts (2006).

Response Options

Beyond thinksheets, we always offer many different choices for kids to respond to their reading: talking, drawing, and writing are all important modes of expression. To create a community of learners, kids often respond to each other's work, adding their thinking to their classmates' posters and products. They also create large murals, self-publish books, write and illustrate poems, and act out stories and concepts. Our long-term goal is to move kids from brief responses to original, more thoughtful ones.

Comprehension Throughout the Day and Across the Curriculum

We don't create Active Literacy Classrooms because they are appealing and fun (though they are) but to empower kids' thinking. Similarly, we don't teach the comprehension strategies as an end in themselves. We hope kids will eventually come to use comprehension strategies as tools for investigating a wide range of topics, issues, and ideas on their own. Their function is to help kids understand what they read in every context, in the literacy block, during reading-writing workshop, in social studies, in science, and beyond.

As David Perkins reminds us, "Knowledge does not just sit there . . . it functions richly in people's lives to help them understand and deal with the world" (1992). Students in Active Literacy Classrooms use comprehension strategies to enhance understanding, learn content, and put their knowledge to work.

Teaching with the *Toolkit*

How to Integrate *The Primary Toolkit* into Your
Reading Program and Your Curriculum

As we visit primary classrooms around the country, we recognize three prevalent models for organizing literacy practices and lessons:

- Reading Workshop
- Balanced Literacy or Guided Reading
- Basal Reading or Scripted Program

Now, of course none of these models are ever completely pure. There is plenty of variation within each approach, and there is often some overlap. Mixed models arise. And, of course, there is always a local flavor to each of them when teachers put these national models to work in living classrooms.

But all the models agree on one thing: an effective reading program must teach comprehension explicitly, directly, and recurrently. The scientific research on this is now incontrovertible and overwhelming (National Reading Panel, 2000). With its explicit approach to comprehension instruction and rich array of resources and guides for teaching, *The Primary Comprehension Toolkit* can be a core element in all three of the models.

Using the *Toolkit* in the Reading Workshop

In a traditional craft workshop, young learners are apprenticed to a master craftsperson and immersed in the real work of the trade. When we apply this approach to literacy instruction in schools, the reading workshop involves much modeling by the teacher, guided practice for the learners, individual coaching and conferring by the veteran practitioner, and the creation of meaningful products (e.g. writings, art work, research reports, social action) aimed at a real audience. Authors and pioneers such as Donald Graves (1991), Shelley Harwayne (2000), Lucy Calkins (1994), Nancy Atwell (1998), and others have taken the reading workshop to a high level of refinement. In many school districts, the workshop model has been adopted as the baseline instructional format for reading and writing.

The essential components of comprehension instruction fit seamlessly into a reading workshop model. In *The Primary Comprehension Toolkit*, we model, thinking out loud as we read to kids and showing them how we think through and respond to text. Next, we guide them to think about text with us as we read and respond to it together. Once kids have a thorough understanding of the task, we send them off to read and respond on their own, with a partner, or in small groups. During independent or collaborative practice, we move around the room conferring with kids in order to provide individualized and differentiated instruction. Instruction is tailored to meet the needs of each and every child. At the end of the workshop, we come back together as a group to share learning and to build a community of learners through conversation and discussions about reading.

The only difference we can see between *PTK* instruction and the reading workshop model is that when we introduce comprehension strategies and practices for the first time, our lessons take longer than standard minilessons. Our lessons are more like "maxilessons" than minilessons, and for good reason. We spend more instructional time modeling and guiding so that we can explicitly teach the reading and thinking strategies. We typically model our own thinking and guide kids through a good portion of text so that they have a clear idea of what to do. Then kids try this out themselves when they are ready. But we don't do *Toolkit* lessons just once. We teach them multiple times in different texts. Subsequent lessons to review and practice thinking strategies can be much shorter, more in the realm of minilessons.

We've found the *Toolkit* lessons especially useful in a reading workshop model because the reading and thinking strategies are cumulative. Kids build a repertoire of these that they apply across many texts and genres. Kids use any and all of the strategies during independent practice. Kids internalize the comprehension strategies as tools they can use to understand whatever they read independently as well as books and articles they discuss in literature circles, inquiry groups, etc. Most importantly, kids come up with a myriad of creative ways to write, think, talk, and draw about their reading.

Using the *Toolkit* with a Balanced Literacy or Guided Reading Program

Most literacy educators agree that a strong reading program must include an array of key activities and experiences, and that it must carefully allocate time among those key elements. Perhaps the best-known models of balanced literacy programs are those described by Fountas and Pinnell (1996) and Cunningham, Hall, and Cunningham (2000). They identify exactly what elements need to be balanced over a day, a week, or a year of instruction. These models so strongly feature small-group instruction using carefully leveled text that "guided reading" often becomes the shorthand label for the whole program.

The Primary Toolkit addresses comprehension instruction within the balanced literacy model. There are countless programs addressing phonics and phonemic awareness, fluency, and other important elements of literacy instruction. We've focused our curriculum on comprehension—to make sure that instruction in this all-important aspect of reading is explicit, robust, and thoughtful.

Within a balanced literacy framework, the modeling and guided practice portions of *Toolkit* lessons are a good fit with instructional read-alouds and shared reading. Kids are up close, and we use large-format text such as big books and posters like the *TFK* posters as we read to and with the children. As we move into the guided practice portion of the lesson, kids often have clipboards so that after we talk and respond together, they write their own responses to leave tracks of their thinking. While they are still up close where we can carefully observe them, we check to see that they are ready to try the task in small groups or on their own.

The Primary Comprehension Toolkit fits like a glove with guided reading practices. *Toolkit* comprehension lessons are perfect for teachers to use as they meet with small guided reading groups. Typically, the guided reading lesson reinforces and reviews a strategy we have taught in a whole-group lesson previously. The small, flexible, needs-based guided reading group provides an opportunity for teachers to design explicit instruction to meet kids' shared learning needs. As kids read in multiple

copies of the same text, we use the Lesson Guide to provide instruction. The Lesson Guide supplies the lesson moves and language that can be applied to any text and works seamlessly with leveled guided reading books. The small guided reading group is ideal for assessing how kids use and apply comprehension strategies as they read, giving teachers a good idea of what to teach next.

Often children who are not meeting with the teacher during guided reading time work collaboratively or independently, usually in centers. As part of center work, we have set up tables with books, Post-its, writing paper, markers, etc., so that kids can use the strategies and response options we have introduced in *Toolkit* lessons. This all-important independent practice focuses kids mainly on reading, with short responses that reinforce the strategy that has been taught. Kids might mark a Post-it with an *L* and record new learning, draw a picture to demonstrate thinking, or ask a question to clarify confusion. The emphasis is on authentic response that contributes to learning rather than responses that simply keep kids busy while the teacher is working with small groups. Kids need to stay busy, but they need to be busy with meaningful work.

Using the *Toolkit* with a Basal Reading or Scripted Program

Most basal programs have plenty of leeway for integrating *Toolkit* comprehension instruction with the selections in the anthology. First of all, anthologies are great sources of additional text for kids. So feel free to use whatever *Toolkit* lesson fits best with selections in the anthology. Also, some users of basal programs have told us that their anthologies lack enough nonfiction to provide kids with solid practice in informational text reading. So integrating the *Toolkit* and its texts with a program provides much-needed, engaging nonfiction for kids.

One thing we have noticed about the comprehension element of many basal reading programs is that although strategies such as asking questions and drawing inferences are mentioned throughout the Teacher's Guide, the basal does not explain how to teach comprehension explicitly. We have yet to see a basal program with robust, in-depth comprehension instruction at its core. Good news! You can't get much more explicit or robust than the *Toolkit* for comprehension instruction. *The Primary Toolkit* gives you both the teaching language and teaching moves to teach a variety of comprehension strategies. So we recommend using the *Toolkit* comprehension lessons to ramp up basal lessons. The Lesson Guides in the six Strategy Books provide an explicit way to teach *Toolkit* comprehension lessons with a basal text.

Beyond the usual range of basal readers, there are some highly scripted programs that leave little time or space for deviation. In that situation, we simply suggest that you use the comprehension curriculum in the *Toolkit* with science and social studies, as we discuss below and on pages 59–64. Many teachers find that teaching comprehension with the potentially fascinating topics of science and social studies not only strengthens kids' reading skills—it often breathes new life into these sometimes neglected corners of the curriculum.

Using the *Toolkit* in All Subject Areas—All Day Long

We're with Howard Gardner, who believes that "The purpose of reading is understanding" (1991). If we don't teach kids to actively use, understand, and remember what they read, what else matters? The *Toolkit* lessons and practices teach kids to "read to learn" as they encounter information and ideas in a wide variety of informational texts.

Comprehension instruction occurs during the literacy block for sure, but also throughout the day, over the course of the year, and in all subject areas. We don't view science or social studies as separate subjects, taught as an after-thought an hour or two a week. We're inclined to agree with David Pearson and researchers from the University of California at Berkeley (2005) that literacy practices should be merged with study in a variety of disciplines, all day and every day. In this way, we support kids to build their background knowledge about the world.

So, science and social studies top the list as opportunities for teaching comprehension in a way that broadens and deepens kids' knowledge about the world. Specific suggestions for integrating comprehension across the curriculum abound in the *Toolkit*. On page 64 you'll find full details about "Using *Toolkit* Components in Science and Social Studies." Strategy Book 6 demonstrates how *Toolkit* instruction can be integrated with a unit of study in science and social studies. And take a look at both the "Reading, Writing, and Research in Science and Social Studies" slideshow and Brad Buhrow's classroom video on the DVD to see how *Toolkit* instruction can reinvigorate neglected or stale content areas.

The Toolkit Components

Teacher's Guide

This 72-page book explains the theory and research that defines comprehension and guides our work. It also provides a quick overview of how to navigate and use the *Toolkit*, explains the teaching-assessing loop, and discusses how the *Toolkit* lessons can be used for teaching across the curriculum.

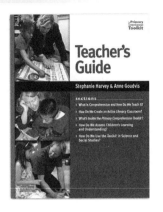

DVD-ROM

The *Toolkit* DVD-ROM provides a wide range of video and print resources to support and enhance your teaching. Whenever you encounter a DVD icon ⊙ in the text, you will know that there is a direct link to materials on the DVD. If you are new to comprehension instruction, we strongly recommend that you view the "Active Literacy Slideshow" and the "Three Classroom Videos" first, to get a look at teachers and kids at work.

This DVD will play in all standard DVD players and on all computers equipped with a DVD drive and playback software. If you are using a computer, the DVD performs optimally when viewed on a Macintosh or when using the WinDVD player on a Windows computer.

The six sections that appear on the Main Menu are:

Active Literacy Slideshow—a narrated slideshow that demonstrates how to create a classroom that promotes active literacy

Component Walkthrough—an animated walkthrough of the *Toolkit* components, their purposes, and how to use them, narrated by the authors

Lesson Walkthrough—an animated walkthrough of the recurring lesson features, narrated by the authors

Comprehension in Action: Three Classroom Videos
- Stephanie Harvey, "Merge Thinking with New Learning"
- Anne Goudvis, "I Learned, I Wonder, Wow!"
- Brad Buhrow (primary teacher), "Content Literacy: Reading, Writing and Research"

Reading, Writing, and Research in Science and Social Studies—A 75-slide presentation about how teachers teach and kids learn to apply comprehension strategies to content area reading. There is no audio in this slideshow.

Electronic Resources—this section of the DVD provides computer users with the key lesson and professional development resources in PDF format. See the onscreen Help for more information. There are three sets of resources in this section.
- **Printable Resources**—PDFs of lesson texts, lesson guides, thinking tools, assessment forms, bibliographies, and the full-color articles from *Keep Reading! A Source Book of Short Text*

- **Research articles**—by leading educators and a co-author

  P. David Pearson and *Nell Duke*, "Comprehension Instruction in the Primary Grades." The authors provide scientifically-based research that supports the explicit teaching of comprehension strategies to children in primary grades.

  Ron Ritchhart and *David Perkins*, "Making Thinking Visible." The authors explain the importance of teaching children to surface, talk about, and share their thinking so they can understand, remember, and use what they learn.

  Nell K. Duke, *V. Susan Bennett-Armistead*, and *Ebony M. Roberts*, "Filling the Great Void—Why We Should Bring Nonfiction into the Early-Grade Classroom." The authors survey classrooms and make a case for filling classrooms with nonfiction texts to expand and build kids' background knowledge of the genre and the world.

  Stephanie Harvey, "Nonfiction Inquiry: Using Real Reading and Writing to Explore the World." The author discusses the myriad ways to integrate nonfiction literacy into the elementary classroom, nurturing kids' passion and curiosity along the way.

- **High Resolution Slideshow**—a high-quality PDF version of the "Reading, Writing, and Research in Science and Social Studies" presentation

Six Strategy Books

At the core of the *Toolkit* are twenty-two lessons grouped into six Strategy Books.

Strategy Book 1: Monitor Comprehension

Strategy Book 2: Activate and Connect

Strategy Book 3: Ask Questions

Strategy Book 4: Infer and Visualize

Strategy Book 5: Determine Importance

Strategy Book 6: Summarize and Synthesize

In each book, you'll find either three or four interconnected lessons for teaching the strategy. Each individual lesson has four elements:

- An **Overview** that previews the purposes, goals, and steps of the lesson.

- The **Lesson in Action**, where you'll see us teach the lesson with a real group of kids so you can study our teaching language and teaching moves.

- Several **Reflect and Assess** pages, showing a range of kids' work and our comments assessing it, as well as ways of adapting the lesson for different groups, grade levels, and individual children in the Adapt and Differentiate section.

- The **Lesson Guide**, a simple template that allows you to teach the lesson yourself, using either our chosen text or your own.

Each Strategy Book features a formal introduction and conclusion. That's because each Strategy Book is really akin to its own cohesive unit, and the six units together create an overarching course of study about active literacy and what it means to wrap your mind around your reading and successfully comprehend. We recommend that you formally introduce each strategy as you begin your study, and formally close it as well. You'll note that each Strategy Wrap-up recommends creating an Anchor Chart that captures the strategy language—the words and phrases that characterize the big ideas of each strategy. As you conclude a strategy study, work with your students to record this language on a chart that you can post in your classroom for easy reference.

Informational Text

Lesson Text Poster Pack

This envelope contains the six *Time For Kids* Bigger Picture Edition posters and *National Geographic Young Explorer* magazine.

Keep Reading! A Source Book of Short Text

We've gathered a collection of compelling text that accompany the lessons. In the *Source Book*, you'll find:

Lesson Text Each of the twenty-two lessons is built around an exemplary text that we've thoroughly tested in classrooms across the country and can guarantee is engaging to students. Much of this text is packaged right in the *Toolkit*: the *Time For Kids* posters and the *National Geographic Young Explorer* magazine. All of those materials are reprinted here in the *Source Book* and are also available as full-color PDFs on the DVD so that you can print them out or make transparencies.

Nonfiction Short Text We love short nonfiction text for introducing kids to strategic reading because it's inherently interesting, engages even the most reluctant readers, and doesn't take long to read. The teachers with whom we work immediately recognize the value of our short nonfiction text and they want to know where they can get their hands on more, more, more! We've made it easy by supplying thirty-nine short pieces specially written for the *Toolkit* on a range of topics that appeal to kids—from nature to families to art, sports, and more. You'll find three levels of text, categorized as most accessible, more challenging, and most challenging. These are very useful for different grade-level applications as well as for differentiation within a single grade level. There's something here for everyone—from the earliest emergent readers and those students who need additional support all the way to your most proficient readers.

Bibliographies As noted earlier, we're always on the lookout for strong, engaging text. Here we share our best sources for finding good text beyond the *Toolkit*—as well as a list of our personal favorites.

Trade and Picture Books This is a list of recently published trade and picture books that we believe will hook kids and pull them into spirited discussions. We have grouped these books into five user-friendly categories: social studies, science, sports, the arts, and literacy.

Magazines for Kids You might be surprised to discover such a rich offering of magazines written and designed especially for kids. Additionally, you'll note that some of our lesson text is pulled from kids' magazines. Some great magazines we recommend for young kids include *National Geographic Young Explorer, TIME For Kids, Weekly Reader,* and the Carus family of magazines, including *Click* and *Ask.*

Exploring Reading Online Sometimes, remarkably engaging, kid-appropriate short text is only a click away. Check out our recommendations for ready-to-use short text you can download from the web as well as great content for kids to read about on their own.

Professional Books and Resources to Extend Your Understanding In keeping with the spirit of *The Primary Comprehension Toolkit*—reading to learn—we've assembled a bibliography of some of the professional books that have enhanced our understanding of reading comprehension process and practice. This isn't a definitive bibliography by any means, but simply a collection of books that have been essential in developing our own understanding of the challenges young readers face and what we can do to support them.

Books that Celebrate the Joy of Reading We do the work we do because, as Bernice Cullinan once wrote, we want to help children "live in the spell of a good book." There are many fine books that celebrate the joys of reading. We include here a list of some of our favorites. We invite you to add your own as a way to keep in mind why we, as educators, must care so passionately about helping children become real readers, who eat, drink, breathe, and live books. Reading changes everything—from the way we view our world to the way we view ourselves. We read not because we're teachers or students, but because we are human beings.

Trade Book Pack (Optional Purchase)

For some lessons, we use diverse and distinctive children's picture books, which we chose for their especially good fit with the specific strategies being taught. You may already have these nine books in your classroom or school library. If not, you might consider purchasing the optional Trade Book Pack. Go to www.comprehensiontoolkit.com for ordering information. Obviously, we treasure these nine cool books and think you will enjoy working with them, but we remind you again that the *Toolkit* gives you all you need to teach the lessons with any texts of your choice. Indeed, that's the whole purpose of the *Toolkit*, to help you develop your own lessons using materials that are just right for your own students. When you introduce kids to the *Toolkit* comprehension strategies, it's important that you use text that naturally appeals to children and will almost certainly captivate them.

How to Teach a *Toolkit* Lesson

As you will see, every *Toolkit* lesson has four parts:

1. The Lesson Overview previews everything you need to know about the lesson: exactly what comprehension strategy is being taught and why, what our goals are for the children, what materials you will need, why we have selected a particular kind of text, and an outline of the teaching steps we will take.

1. The Lesson Overview

2. The Lesson in Action is like a demonstration lesson you might observe in a classroom. You'll follow along as one of us teaches a specific comprehension strategy to a real class of kids, using a carefully chosen piece of text. As you read the interplay between us and the children, you can notice the steps, the language, and the trajectory of the lesson as it unfolds. You'll also see the side comments and suggestions we placed in the margin as we reflected on the lesson ourselves.

All 22 lessons have a consistent structure:

CONNECT and ENGAGE   First, we **engage** kids in the lesson and **connect** them to the text.

MODEL   Then, we **model** a comprehension strategy for children.

GUIDE   Next, we help kids **practice the strategy with our direct guidance**.

COLLABORATE or PRACTICE INDEPENDENTLY   When they are ready, we ask children to **practice the strategy collaboratively or independently**, while we work with individuals or small invitational groups.

SHARE THE LEARNING   Finally, we get together again at the end of the lesson to **share the learning**, and lay the groundwork for the next lesson.

So, the **Lesson in Action** is our way of showing you the teaching language and teaching moves we use when we teach kids. The **Lesson in Action** is not a script for you to follow as you teach the lesson. It is a snapshot of the teaching and learning in one classroom at one particular time and place. Read the **Lesson in Action** to yourself ahead of time, studying how the moves and language played out with those kids, and then teach using the Lesson Guide. (See below).

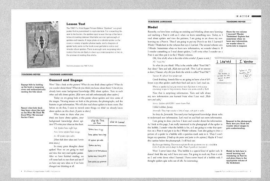

2. The Lesson in Action

3. The Reflect and Assess section shows how we track kids' thinking by studying the naturally occurring artifacts of *Toolkit* teaching—drawings, writings, Post-it notes, thinksheets, and charts—as well as by listening carefully and making notes on kids' questions, conversations, and presentations. The **Adapt and Differentiate** section explores how we differentiate instruction for emergent readers, more developed readers, and avid readers. We also share strategies for adapting the lesson to children learning English.

3. The Reflect and Assess section

4. The Lesson Guide is the most important tool of all. It is the template for your own teaching. The **Lesson Guide** contains all the same steps we used in our Lesson In Action demonstration, including our prompts, comments, and questions for the children. But the **Lesson Guide** is written in generic language so you can recreate our lesson with your own kids and your own text. The **Lesson Guide** might sit on your lap as a cheat sheet to help you along. The first time teachers teach a strategy, they often use our chosen lesson text. But later, when kids need more instruction or practice, teachers use the **Lesson Guide** to create another engaging lesson. The *Primary Toolkit* lessons were not created as one-shot lessons, but rather as lessons to be taught multiple times with different texts and in different subject areas, as the need arises.

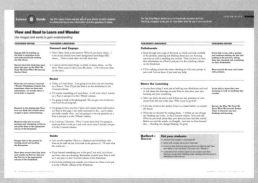

4. The Lesson Guide

The **Primary** Comprehension **Toolkit**

Lesson Titles and Lesson Texts

Lesson Number and Title	*Lesson Text and Author*

	Lesson Number and Title	Lesson Text and Author

Book 4

Infer & Visualize

12 Infer Meaning
Merge background knowledge with clues from the text

Honey, I Love
and other love poems
by Eloise Greenfield

13 Learn to Visualize
Get a picture in your mind

Honey, I Love
and other love poems
by Eloise Greenfield

14 Make Sense of New Information
Infer from features, pictures, and words

"Ladybugs Grow Up"
TIME For kids

15 Infer and Visualize with Narrative Nonfiction
Tie thinking to the text

Antarctica
by Helen Cowcher

Book 5

Determine Importance

16 Figure Out What's Important
Separate important information from interesting details

"Amazing Helen Keller"
TIME For Kids

17 Paraphrase Information
Merge your thinking to make meaning

"A Visit to Mexico"
TIME For Kids

18 Organize your Thinking as You Read
Take notes to record information

"Welcome to the Rain Forest"
TIME For Kids

Book 6

Summarize & Synthesize

19 Summarize Information
Put it in your own words and keep it interesting

"Welcome to the Rain Forest"
TIME For Kids

20 Read to Get the Big Ideas
Synthesize the text

The Great Kapok Tree
by Lynne Cherry

21 Explore and Investigate
Read, write, and draw in researcher's workshop

"Welcome to the Rain Forest"
TIME For Kids
The Great Kapok Tree
by Lynne Cherry

22 Share Your Learning
Create projects to demonstrate understanding

Student work
A variety of texts on the project topic

We find it helpful to envision each *Toolkit* lesson as four interrelated parts: Lesson Overview, Lesson in Action, Reflect and Assess, and Lesson Guide. This walkthrough provides an explanation of the features and benefits of each part.

Lesson Overview

This is the Overview page, the opening spread. The recurring features on this page establish the instructional framework for all twenty-two lessons by listing the resources needed, stating the purpose, and identifying the Gradual Release plan.

Title and subtitle clue you in to the strategy and the activity focus of the lesson.

The photographs show us at work in real classrooms where we developed and used the lessons.

Text Matters tells you what kind of text we chose for this particular strategy lesson. We offer tips for finding appropriate books, articles, posters, and other reading materials that will work when you teach this lesson yourself, using the Lesson Guide (see pages 46–47).

What materials do you need to assemble in order to enjoy a successful teaching experience? We list them here and recommend you gather what you need before you start teaching.

Lesson **8**

View and Read to Learn and Wonder

Text Matters

When teaching readers to connect new information to what they already know, we search for text on a familiar and intriguing topic that is also likely to contain ideas that kids don't already know. It is the fresh information that lends itself to wondering. Questions come quickly on the heels of new facts and concepts. As kids activate background knowledge to better understand new information, they may come to see that they have prior misconceptions, which reading and learning can reverse. As always with primary kids, we make sure to choose text with compelling images, so that they are more apt to pay attention, notice new information, and wonder about it.

Resources & Materials

Lesson Text
TIME For Kids Bigger Picture Edition [Fall 2002] "Spiders!" poster

Classroom Supplies
- *What We Think We Know/What We Learned* Anchor Chart and marker
- Post-its

Student Supplies
- Clipboard with *I Learned/I Wonder* Thinksheet and Post-its or *Post-its* Thinksheets [See *Strategy Book 3*, pages 67–69, or the DVD-ROM.]
- Student copy of "Spiders" [See *Keep Reading! A Source Book of Short Text*, pages 5–8 or the DVD-ROM]
- Assorted markers, pencils, and crayons

2   The Primary Comprehension Toolkit: Ask Questions

1. Lesson Overview
Launches the lesson with
an instructional framework

2. Lesson in Action

3. Reflect & Assess

4. Lesson Guide

LESSON OVERVIEW

Header information tells you which part
of the lesson you are viewing.

Use images and words to gain understanding

Goals& Assessment

We want students to:

- use text and images to understand.
- think and wonder about new learning.
- jot down new learning and questions on Post-its and then sort them in two columns: *I Learned* and *I Wonder.*
- understand that misconceptions are normal and that learners revise their thinking after reading and listening to additional information.

How

Connect and Engage
- Engage kids by holding up the book or magazine cover and enthusiastically reading the title aloud.
- Record what kids think they know about the topic on the *What We Think We Know/What We Learned* Anchor Chart.

Model
- Share the two-column *I Learned/I Wonder* Thinksheet. Explain that sometimes when we learn new information, we wonder about it. Invite kids to respond.
- Respond to the photograph. Show how you think and wonder about images to gain understanding.
- Model for kids how to record learning and wondering on Post-its and place them in the appropriate column of the thinksheet.

Guide
- Engage kids in the process by reading aloud and guiding the discussion.
- Have them record what they learn and wonder on Post-its, then put the Post-its in the appropriate column of the thinksheet.

Collaborate
- Invite kids to join with a partner and continue reading the text and looking at the pictures, jotting their new learning and wondering on their thinksheets.
- Move around the room and confer with partners.

Share the Learning
- Invite kids to share their new learning as well as anything they wonder.
- Review the *What We Think We Know/What We Learned* Anchor Chart to discover any new thinking and learning.

Why& What

Background knowledge is the primary determinant of comprehension. Nonfiction reading in particular requires readers to think about what they know in order to understand new information. So we encourage kids to ask questions about new information to make sure they understand it. In this lesson, kids use a thinksheet titled *I Learned/I Wonder* to support understanding as they meet new information while reading. Sometimes young children have limited or inaccurate background knowledge and develop misconceptions. In this lesson, we create a class Anchor Chart titled *What We Think We Know/What We Learned* before we read about the new topic. Then after reading, we go back and notice whether what we thought we knew was accurate and we celebrate how reading changes thinking and clears up prior misconceptions.

Lesson 8: View and Read to Learn and Wonder   3

What's the point of the lesson? What do we want our students to learn? Goals and Assessment lists our goals for teaching and learning and links them to Reflect and Assess.

What do you do and how do you it? The How feature explains every teaching move you'll make. These prompts form the basis of the Gradual Release of Responsibility framework.

Why do we recommend this lesson and what does it entail? Here you get a quick explanation of the theory behind the practice.

Lesson in Action

In keeping with the Gradual Release of Responsibility framework, the Lesson in Action showcases our modeling and guided practice for each lesson. We invite you to enter our lesson and watch us teach, listen to our language, watch our teaching moves, and see the ways in which our students respond to the text we are reading and discussing. Additionally, on the borders running alongside the Lesson in Action, you can read our ongoing commentary. Consider those remarks to be akin to the voice-overs you might hear on a video: we comment on the lesson itself and offer additional teaching tips to help you teach the lesson more effectively.

The Lesson in Action is a sample or demonstration lesson. The Lesson Guide (coming up on pages 46–47) is your tool for teaching the lesson with any text you choose.

Information about the specific text used in this lesson is included here.

The side column provides you with our Teaching Moves, showing the Gradual Release of Responsibility Framework in practice.

The main column describes in detail our Teaching Language and how we bring comprehension instruction to life.

Lesson Text

The *TIME For Kids* Bigger Picture Edition "Spiders!" is a great poster that is guaranteed to captivate kids. For connecting the new to the known, the spiders topic is near the top of the list in terms of creating interest. Most kids just can't get enough of spiders and insects. A large photo of a colorful spider on the cover, a variety of spider photos inside, and a diagram of spider body parts on the back cover get kids to notice and wonder about spiders. There is enough new, surprising information that we are likely to clear up a misconception or two in the process of reading this article.

Used with permission from *TIME For Kids*.

TEACHING MOVES	TEACHING LANGUAGE

Connect and Engage

Engage kids by holding up the book or magazine cover and enthusiastically reading the title aloud.

Wow! Take a look at this picture! What do you think about spiders? What do you wonder about them? What do you think you know about them? A lot of you already have some background knowledge (BK) about spiders. Turn to each other and talk about spiders. *[Kids turn and talk enthusiastically about spiders.]*

Today we are going look at this poster about spiders and view some of the images. Viewing means we look at the pictures, the photographs, and the features to get information. We will also read about spiders to learn more. But before we do that, I want to record some things we *think* we already know about spiders on this chart. *[I point to chart.]*

Record what kids think they know about the topic on the *What We Think We Know/What We Learned* Anchor Chart.

Who wants to share what you think you know about spiders, your background knowledge about spiders? I'll write your ideas on the chart.

Ted: Spiders have eight legs.

Ann: Some spiders have wings.

Jo: All spiders spin webs.

[More kids share ideas and I write them down.]

So many great thoughts about spiders! Now we are going to read and view this very cool spider poster. After we have finished reading, we will come back to our chart and see if we have any new ideas or if we have changed our thinking at all.

What We Think We Know	What We Learned
Spiders have 8 legs.	
Some spiders have wings.	
All spiders spin webs.	
Spiders are hairy.	
Spiders do not have antennas.	
Spiders have 3 body parts.	
Some spiders are poisonous.	

4   The Primary Comprehension Toolkit: Ask Questions

Toolkit's   **Four-Part Lesson Structure**

1. **Lesson Overview**
2. **Lesson in Action**
   Lets you watch Steph and Anne teach
3. **Reflect & Assess**
4. **Lesson Guide**

IN ACTION

TEACHING LANGUAGE	TEACHING MOVES

Model

Recently, we have been working on noticing and thinking about new learning and marking a Post-it with an *L* when we learn something new. Today, as I read about spiders and view the pictures, I am going to jot down my new learning on a Post-it. Then I am going to put my Post-it on this *I Learned/I Wonder* Thinksheet in the column that says *I Learned*. The second column says *I Wonder*. Sometimes when we learn new information, we wonder about it. If I wonder something as I read about spiders, I will write what I wonder on a Post-it and then put it in the *I Wonder* column.

OK, first of all, what is the title of this article? *[I point to title.]*

All: "Feed Me."

So what do you think? Why is the article called "Feed Me"? Any ideas? Turn and talk. *[Kids turn and talk. Then I call on someone to share.]* Tanner, why did you think the article is called "Feed Me"?

Tanner: It's about how spiders eat.

Good thinking. Sounds like we are going to learn a lot of different ways that spiders catch their food and eat it. Let's read on:

When a spider is hungry, watch out! Spiders have many amazing ways to trap insects. Some can even catch a fish!

Now that is surprising information. Turn and talk about any new information you learned from what I just read. *[Kids turn and talk.]*

Jenny: Spiders catch fish! I never knew that.

I didn't either, Jenny.

Jeremiah: They trap insects in lots of ways, not just in webs.

So they do, Jeremiah. You used your background knowledge about webs to understand new information. Let's read on and find out more information.

I am going to show you how I learn and wonder about the information. As I look at this page, I am really interested in the photograph of the spider in this bubble. I *wonder* what the bubble is for, so I am going to write that question on a Post-it and put it in the *I Wonder* column. I am also going to draw a picture of a spider in a bubble with a question mark next to it. Then I won't forget my question. *[I hold up the poster and point to the caption.]* Maybe if I read this caption below the photograph, I will find out:

Spiders go fishing. The water spider floats underwater in a bubble web. It sticks out its legs to fish. Then it pulls in its meal.

Wow! I never knew that. This bubble is a special kind of spider web. It doesn't look like any web I have ever seen. I'm going to mark my Post-it with an *L* and write down what I learned. I have never heard of a bubble web. I thought spiders spin webs out of silk. So interesting.

Teaching Moves column:

Share the two-column *I Learned/I Wonder* Thinksheet. Explain that sometimes when we learn new information, we wonder about it. Invite kids to respond.

Respond to the photograph. Show how you think and wonder about images to gain understanding.

Model for kids how to record learning and wondering on Post-its and place them in the appropriate column of the thinksheet.

Side annotations:

The Teaching Moves listed in the Overview are repeated here for you, at point of use.

The charts we co-construct with students are shown in progress.

In brackets, we describe what we are doing—similar to stage directions.

Footer information tells you the lesson number and title.

Reflect & Assess

Have you ever wondered what we do with all those drawings, writings, and Post-its our kids generate? We study them! These artifacts—along with anchor charts, thinksheets, and student conversations—provide that all-important window into our students' learning. By reading the visible evidence of their thinking and hearing what our kids have to say, we get a clear picture of what they're understanding—and what's not coming across for them as well. With this knowledge in hand, we know what to teach and how to teach it so we can custom-fit sensitive instruction to every child, which is, of course, the essence of responsive teaching.

The Goals and Assessment list from the Overview page is turned into questions here so you can reflect on outcomes as you assess student work.

Reflect and Assess tells you how we look at kids' work for this lesson and assess new progress.

This section gives you ideas for how to tailor the lesson to fit the needs of the whole range of learners in your classroom.

REFLECT & ASSESS

Did your students:

- use text and images to understand?
- think and wonder about new learning?
- jot down new learning and questions on Post-its and then sort them in two columns: *I Learned* and *I Wonder*?
- understand that misconceptions are normal and that learners revise their thinking after reading and listening to additional information?

Reflect & Assess

The *I Learned/I Wonder* Thinksheet is one of the most popular tools we use with primary kids because a question often follows quickly on the heels of new learning. As we review the thinksheets from this lesson, we look for Post-its marked with L and any questions that come from that new learning. Sometimes, learners have a question directly related to new information. They may even connect it with an arrow. Other times, learners jot down a question that emerges as they read and explore a topic.

Adapt & Differentiate

This lesson was done with first graders, but here are suggestions for how to adapt and differentiate for the whole range of learners.

First graders place their Post-its on the *I Learned/I Wonder* form. We nudge second graders to write directly on the thinksheet, although, if it helps them to organize their thinking to use Post-its when they first try it, they are welcome to do that as well. For kindergarteners, we use a larger 11x17 thinksheet and 3x5 Post-its to give them extra room to draw and write. In this lesson we introduce the notion of wondering. Second graders and many first graders are generally familiar with the term *wonder* and understand that it is related to asking questions. With younger learners and English-language learners, we often need to spend time modeling what it is to wonder and we teach the language explicitly.

Lesson 8: View and Read to Learn and Wonder   9

1. **Lesson Overview**

2. **Lesson in Action**

3. **Reflect & Assess**
   Illustrates Anne and Steph's strategies for monitoring student progress

4. **Lesson Guide**

REFLECT & ASSESS ▬

Thinksheets

I Learned | I Wonder

Ⓡ I nvr new spidrs can Jump.

Haw Ds spdr cch fish ?

Ⓛ some spidrs work in grops and make Big webs

I wonDer wht thay (cach)?

camlflsh

Do spidrs have wings?

2 This thinksheet shows active reading and learning. The student also connected his question to new learning with an arrow. I was confused by the Post-it in the bottom left-hand corner, so I conferred with the student. He showed me on the *TIME For Kids* "Spiders!" poster where a spider uses camouflage, a concept he already understood, and explained that many animals use camouflage as protection against enemies, not just spiders.

Lesson 8: View and Read to Learn and Wonder   11

Blank versions of all the thinksheets used in lessons are available on the *The Primary Comprehension Toolkit DVD-ROM* and at the back of the respective Strategy Books.

We include actual student work samples so that you can see the results of the lesson. The work samples may be in the form of Post-its, charts, drawings, two-column forms, or lengthier written responses. Student work includes examples from children who demonstrate understanding as well as those who need more practice.

These captions and annotations explain what we see as we assess student work and can give you direction for how to confer with your own students about their work.

Lesson Guide

The Lesson Guide is a distillation of the Lesson in Action. You can copy it, hold it on your lap if you'd like, and use it to guide you along. We have designed the Lesson Guide generically so that you can teach with the *Toolkit* Lesson Text or any text of your choosing. The Lesson Guide shows you specific teaching language and teaching moves—a kind of "cheat sheet" to help you along the way. Because we focus on teaching the reader, not merely the reading, the strategy instruction in each lesson can be applied to a wide range of text.

The Gradual Release of Responsibility framework headings give the lesson its overall structure.

All the Teaching Moves from the lessons appear together to serve as the foundation for your instruction.

The Teaching Language suggests ways you can guide kids through each step of the lesson—written in generic language that can be used with any text.

Lesson 8 Guide Use this Lesson Guide and any text of your choice to teach students to notice and record new information and the questions it raises.

View and Read to Learn and Wonder

Use images and words to gain understanding

TEACHING MOVES	TEACHING LANGUAGE
	Connect and Engage
Engage kids by holding up the book or magazine cover and enthusiastically reading the title aloud.	▪ Wow! Take a look at this picture! What do you know about…? A lot of you already have some background knowledge (BK) about…. Turn to each other and talk about that.
Record what kids think they know about the topic on the *What We Think We Know/What We Learned* Anchor Chart.	▪ I want to record some things we think we know about…on this chart. Who wants to share your BK about…? I'll write your ideas on the chart.
	Model
Share the two-column *I Learned/ I Wonder* Thinksheet. Explain that sometimes when we learn new information, we wonder about it. Invite kids to respond.	▪ Today, as I read about…I am going to jot down my new learning on a Post-it. Then I'll put the Post-it on this thinksheet in the *I Learned* column.
	▪ If I wonder something as I read about…I will write what I wonder on a Post-it and put it in the *I Wonder* column.
	▪ I'm going to look at the photograph. We can get a lot of information from the photograph.
Respond to the photograph. Show how you think and wonder about images to gain understanding.	▪ I'm going to show you how I learn and wonder about information as I look at this page. I am really interested in the…and it makes me really wonder what…so I am going to write my question on a Post-it and put it in the *I Wonder* column.
Model for kids how to record learning and wondering on Post-its and place them in the appropriate column of the thinksheet.	▪ As I read on, I discover…Wow! I never knew that! I'm going to mark my Post-it with an *L* and write down what I learned and put it in the *I Learned* column.
	Guide
Engage kids in the process by reading aloud and guiding the discussion.	▪ Let's try this together. Here is a clipboard and thinksheet with Post-its for each of you. Let's look at the picture of…I'll read what the words say….
Have them record what they learn and wonder on Post-its, then put the Post-its in the appropriate column of the thinksheet.	▪ If you learned something new in the part I just read, jot it down and draw your new learning. Remember to mark your Post-it with an *L* and put it in the *I Learned* column of the thinksheet.
	▪ If you have anything you wonder, jot it down on a Post-it and put it in the *I Wonder* column of the thinksheet.

14   The Primary Comprehension Toolkit: Ask Questions

1. Lesson Overview

2. Lesson in Action

3. Reflect & Assess

4. Lesson Guide
   Outlines the lesson's teaching
   moves and language

The Teaching Moves outline your instructional sequence and the
Teaching Language gives you an idea about what to say to your students.

LESSON GUIDE

TEACHING LANGUAGE	TEACHING MOVES
Collaborate	
▪ Read through your copy of the book or article and look carefully at the pictures, noticing and thinking about any new learning you have as well as anything you wonder. Then jot down or draw that information on a Post-it and put it in the matching column on the thinksheet.	Invite kids to join with a partner and continue reading the text and looking at the pictures, jotting their new learning and wondering on their thinksheets.
▪ I'll be walking around the room, checking in with your groups as you work. Let me know if you need any help!	Move around the room and confer with partners.
Share the Learning	
▪ As you share today, I want you to hold up your thinksheet and read or talk about the drawings on your Post-its that show your new learning and your wondering.	Invite kids to share their new learning as well as anything they wonder.
▪ After you share, be sure to ask if there are any questions or comments from the rest of the class. Who wants to go first?	
▪ Let's take a look at the Anchor Chart we created before we started the lesson.	Review the *What We Think We Know/What We Learned* Anchor Chart to discover any new thinking and learning.
▪ What did we discover by reading about…? I think we can change our thinking and write…in the *I Learned* column. Turn and talk. What do you think about that, now that you have read the article? Before we read the article, we thought…and now we have learned that…. Reading can change thinking. So great.	

Reflect& Assess

Did your students:
- use text and images to understand?
- think and wonder about new learning?
- jot down new learning and questions on Post-its and then sort them in two columns: *I Learned* and *I Wonder?*
- understand that misconceptions are normal and that learners revise their thinking after reading and listening to additional information?

Lesson Goals and Assessment appear
again so you can remember to teach
with the end in mind.

Lesson 8: View and Read to Learn and Wonder   15

Choosing and Using Text
for *Toolkit* Instruction

As we have been emphasizing, the big payoff of *Toolkit* teaching comes when you develop your own lessons, using text you have chosen just for your kids. You may use one of our Lesson Guides and follow the basic structure of that lesson—or you may launch off on your own, picking a great book and inviting kids to read and think through a unique series of steps you create.

But right now, we will get a little more specific about the review process we follow when choosing text for kids.

Think Through the Text Ahead of Time

We carefully read through and think about text before using it with kids. We need to consider our purpose for teaching with a specific piece of text and how the selection supports instruction. We consider how the selection lends itself to teaching a particular strategy. We also need to troubleshoot obstacles that we anticipate may cause confusion. When launching a strategy practice or lesson, we choose interesting, accessible text that we think will engage our kids. As they become more practiced in a particular strategy, we support them to use the strategy with more challenging and less considerate text.

Encourage Flexibility

The *Toolkit* is designed to teach readers to be flexible and adapt their reading strategies to a variety of text. The *Toolkit* lessons teach kids to read a wide range of nonfiction text, including picture books, trade books, magazine articles, poems, textbooks, and web articles.

Make sure to consider your own curriculum and your students' needs when you select text. Remember all the diverse possibilities for nonfiction. Where we have chosen a magazine feature article for a *Toolkit* lesson, you might choose a different magazine article. Where we have chosen expository nonfiction, you may want to substitute with another expository piece. In several of the lessons, we use narrative picture books. As an alternative, you might choose a narrative picture book about a topic you are studying. If we use a poem to infer meaning, we invite you to try one of your favorite poems for the same purpose.

We recognize that all text, genres, and forms foster a wide range of thinking. Without a doubt, we monitor our comprehension, determine importance, and try to synthesize meaning with any piece of text we pick up. But we also find that some text types lend themselves especially well to a particular strategy or two for the purpose of instruction. Here are some brief guidelines for finding texts that support the teaching of specific strategies.

Activating and Connecting to Background Knowledge

We choose text that kids are likely to have some prior knowledge about. Topics such as pets, family, school, and common childhood experiences are a good bet. When kids read text on familiar topics, they are more likely to connect new information to that which they already know in order to construct meaning.

Questioning: We choose text that sparks wonder and inquiry. Texts and topics for which readers lack background knowledge often spur them to ask questions.

Inferring: We choose text that is ambiguous and nudges the readers to think about what they know. By merging their thinking with clues in the text, they make an inference or draw a conclusion.

Visualizing: We choose vivid text in which the writer paints pictures with the words and uses active verbs and specific nouns to show rather than merely tell the story or information.

Above all, we teach our kids to develop and use a full repertoire of comprehension strategies actively and flexibly in every text they read, listen to, or view.

Scheduling the *Toolkit* into the
Day, Week, and Year

Recall that the *Toolkit* is not an add-on, something extra you have to shoehorn in to your schedule every day. Instead, the *Toolkit* replaces less powerful instructional practices that foster simple recall of facts rather than deep understanding. *PTK* fosters asking questions that lead to new learning. When you use the *Toolkit*, you are offering much more robust comprehension instruction—experiences that truly help your students become lifelong learners. The skills they'll learn from working with the *Toolkit* will help them develop strategic, active literacy skills they can use with any text. This work is most definitely worth a good chunk of classroom time, every day.

In order to teach all six comprehension strategies, we focus on one strategy for several lessons and then move on to another. But the ultimate goal is a fluid, seamless use of all six strategies. We want kids to spontaneously choose and use the strategies that will help them read their way into full comprehension.

So, for first- and second-graders, we recommend that you introduce all six Strategy Books, comprising twenty-two lessons, within the first twenty to twenty-six weeks of the school year. This promptly engages kids in the entire set of comprehension strategies. They can begin using them simultaneously across a range of text. For the first two to four weeks, we recommend that you not jump into the lessons. Rather, offer children an intensive "marinating period," during which you immerse them in the world of books and especially the joys of nonfiction. For details on this important preliminary work, please look back at the "Getting Started with Nonfiction" section on pages 9–11. You are the best judge of how much marinating your kids need—one week, four weeks, or no weeks—to get them ready for formal comprehension instruction.

Many kindergarten teachers prefer to spend the whole first semester in an extended "falling-in-love-with-books" experience—something like our marinating period systematically stretched out. During that fall semester, kindergarten teachers not only immerse kids in a rich experience of all genres of text, teaching them to think when they are listening and viewing. But they also work on phonemic awareness, phonics, and word study skills. This helps kids break the sound/symbol code and move toward fluent reading. Then, they more formally launch *Toolkit* teaching in the second semester, following the same pattern we use with the older kids. Still other kindergarten teachers are entirely comfortable launching the *Toolkit* comprehension instruction at the start of the year. We use the six strategies in listening and viewing as well as in reading, so even very emergent readers have opportunities to think.

Flexibility Is the Key

When it comes to scheduling and instruction, *flexibility* is our mantra! While we have placed the lessons in a suggested order, what is most important is that your kids' learning needs drive your instruction. To us, the idea of sequence is mainly one of language being introduced and used. Yes, a few lessons do work well in order, often because they were designed as two-day, two-part experiences. For example, if you introduce nonfiction features with Lesson 2, it makes sense to move directly to Lesson 3, where kids write their own nonfiction feature books on subsequent days.

But mainly, we don't want you locked into a sequence but do want you empowered to meet your kids' needs as developing thinkers, wherever they are. These are not so much one-time lessons as ongoing practices. After all, readers do not "discover their passion" only once!

If you know your kids well and are clear about your purpose for teaching, you can use the *Toolkit* quite flexibly, dipping in and out of the Strategy Books and focusing on the specific strategies that your students most need to learn at a particular point. So, if your students are experienced in activating and connecting new information to what they already know, they may not need to go through all of the lessons in that Strategy Book. On the other hand, if your kids are struggling with a particular strategy, you might want to teach every lesson in that Strategy Book and provide lots of extra practice to support kids as they read.

If your kids are new to a particular strategy, we recommend that you teach all of the lessons in that book to give them a solid grounding in that strategy. And, usually, it will help to teach the lessons in order within the book, because they are cumulative.

One caveat, in our opinion, deserves to be mentioned: monitoring comprehension is much more than a strategy. It is a thinking disposition that enables readers to keep track of their thinking and understanding and to be aware of their reading process. It is this awareness that allows them to make connections, ask questions, or draw inferences that result in understanding. It is difficult to be strategic if we are unaware or not paying to attention to our thinking when reading, listening, or viewing. So, we strongly suggest that you either introduce or review the monitoring comprehension strategy before you jump into one of the other *Toolkit* Strategy Books.

Using *Toolkit* Lessons with Different Literacy Models

As we teach comprehension and thinking strategies with *The Primary Toolkit*, we design a schedule that reflects the way we deliver literacy in our classrooms. Here's what that time-sharing might look like as we integrate *Toolkit* instruction with reader's workshop, balanced literacy, and basal programs—and across the curriculum.

Reader's Workshop
In reader's workshop, we launch *Toolkit* lessons during the modeling and guided practice portion of the workshop. We spend a longer block of time (a "maxi" lesson) showing kids how to use a strategy and guiding them through texts. Once we've launched the strategy, our follow-up minilessons tend to be five-to-ten minutes long. Kids can then work with a partner or independently to practice on their own with self-selected text or text at their level that we suggest. They draw, write, and discuss all manner of responses. At the same time, collaborative or

independent work time is the perfect opportunity to pull needs-based, flexible small groups for targeted instruction on specific strategies for kids who need additional guidance from a teacher.

For Example: In one kindergarten we know well, the kids spend several weeks at the beginning of the year "marinating" in nonfiction of all varieties, the classroom awash in nonfiction. The teacher conducts minilessons in nonfiction literacy, modeling her thinking and then sending kids off to practice on their own. Tubs of nonfiction books cover the tables. Post-its, pencils, and markers are readily available for kids to draw something they learned or mark a spot where they wondered with a question mark as the teacher moves around the room conferring with them. Each day at the culmination of the workshop, kids share out at the circle.

Every week or so, the teacher introduces a Primary Toolkit *strategy in a longer launch lesson and then reviews that same strategy in her minilessons over subsequent days. For instance, kids spend two full weeks learning about different features, making a class Feature/Purpose book, noticing features in books, and beginning to use features as they draw information they are learning. As the kids are introduced to the idea of noticing new learning, they continue using features in their responses.* Toolkit *instruction in this classroom is about writing as much as reading, so in the workshop each day, kids talk, draw, and write, using invented spellings and their growing knowledge of sound/symbol correspondence to record their new learning. Most important, the kids keep using the strategies they have already practiced on a daily basis during reading workshop.*

Balanced Literacy/Guided Reading

We launch *Toolkit* lessons during shared reading time, modeling and guiding kids to think through shared text such as the *Toolkit* trade books, *TFK* posters, or other picture books or big books. We launch a *Toolkit* strategy with shared text in either a large-group launch lesson or a teacher-directed small group lesson. Either works just fine. During the time when kids are reading on their own in leveled text, they

practice using the newly introduced comprehension strategy, as well as previously taught strategies. We also set up centers that focus on strategic reading and thinking—providing kids with Post-its, thinksheets, and other scaffolds so they can write and draw using the strategies they have learned with whatever text they are reading.

For Example: One school uses the Toolkit *in their balanced literacy program. After teaching all of the kids the lessons in the Monitor Comprehension Strategy Book, the teachers teach* Toolkit *lessons in small, needs-based guided reading groups. The school is steeped in comprehension strategy instruction, so some second-graders, for instance, already have a strong foundation in making connections and questioning in nonfiction text. So the teacher begins* Toolkit *instruction for them with the Infer & Visualize Strategy Book. Other guided reading groups may be working on activating and connecting to background knowledge or asking questions, depending on their needs.*

For Example: A team of first-grade teachers work together to plan out Toolkit *instruction over the first months of the school year. Kids are already familiar with nonfiction as a genre, so the teachers introduce one* Toolkit *lesson at the beginning of each week. The launch lesson is completed in one longer block, and after the teacher models, the kids spend much of the first day in guided practice with partners in the meeting area. In this way, the teachers observe everyone as they confer with kids, making sure kids understand the strategy and are ready to try it on their own. Teachers note those kids who need additional small-group practice so they can review the lesson in small, flexible needs-based guided reading groups on subsequent days.*

The following day, after a brief minilesson to review the strategy, kids disperse to centers to practice the strategy with nonfiction books at their respective levels. At each center, teachers place an example of responses based on lessons taught previously—a sample Post-it marked with a ? or an L, or phrases that kids might use in their written response, such as "I wonder . . . " or "I learned." Centers are set up so that kids can be as independent as possible while the teachers pull small groups for instruction. Small-group guided reading lessons include review of strategies already introduced at the beginning of the week. Lessons are adapted to the needs of different groups, so that instruction is differentiated.

At the end of the guided reading session, each class comes together to share their learning—in this way the teachers can make a quick assessment of what kids accomplish independently in the centers.

Basal Program

We launch comprehension lessons using a *Toolkit* trade book or a *Time For Kids* poster. Or we can substitute a basal selection that works well to launch a particular strategy or *Toolkit* practice. Another approach is to use the *Toolkit* text to introduce a strategy or practice initially and then use the same strategy with a selection from the basal anthology the very next day. Since basal selections are often quite lengthy, we begin the selection using a particular strategy lesson. Then kids continue to use the strategy they've been taught as they finish reading the selection. When working with additional short texts—regardless of whether they're part of a basal program or leveled text we've chosen—kids continue to use the strategies we've taught so that they get plenty of that all-important independent reading time.

For Example: In one district, teachers use their whole ninety-minute literacy block every Friday to teach a full Toolkit *strategy lesson. Then, on the following Monday*

through Thursday, kids practice the featured comprehension strategy in selections from the basal. They also do the skill sections of the basal program. When Friday comes around, another ninety-minute Toolkit lesson immerses kids in thinking and sets the pace for the following week. This plan evolved because the district recognized that the comprehension instruction in the basal program was too limited to grow powerful readers who use comprehension strategies to understand what they read.

Science and Social Studies

Many schools and teachers use the *Toolkit* across the curriculum, expanding into science and social studies. Often teachers using highly scripted reading programs simply make the content areas the home of strong comprehension instruction, using the nonfiction topics and materials these potentially fascinating subjects offer kids. On pages 59–64 we explain in more detail how you can use *Toolkit* lessons and materials across the curriculum.

For Example: In one second-grade classroom, Toolkit *strategies are introduced as an integral part of science and social studies instruction. As the teachers plan the required weather curriculum study, they incorporate* Toolkit *instruction, which they continue to use in subsequent social studies and science units throughout the year. To build background knowledge, kids read and respond to a variety of nonfiction, including books, charts, videos, maps, newspaper articles, and online sources. Kids notice new information and ask questions as they read and view all these different sources. They write and draw what they are learning, using features such as close-ups, labels, and captions.*

Toolkit lessons focusing on both note-taking and summarizing and synthesizing information provide ways for kids to organize the information they are learning and create books, poems, posters, and other projects to share knowledge. In this way, reading, writing, and thinking strategies become a means to an end—investigating new topics as kids learn about the real world.

Sample Weekly Toolkit Lesson Schedule

The Primary Toolkit has been designed with flexibility in mind. Rather than "the almighty schedule," your kids' learning needs and interests drive instruction. We have outlined the following suggestions simply to provide ideas for planning and discussion. And of course, *Toolkit* lessons are cumulative, so as we introduce and launch new lessons, we make sure kids continue to use those strategies they already have under their belts.

The *Toolkit* emphasizes reading, writing, talking, listening, and investigating, all of which are essential practices that promote active learning and lead to successful comprehension across a range of texts. The *Toolkit* enables students to use the comprehension strategies independently in their own reading as well as in *Toolkit* text.

Indeed, once we complete a strategy, we recommend that kids spend some time applying what they have learned to real-world reading. They can read and practice *Toolkit* strategies in their own self-selected text. They can read magazines and newspapers. They can try an entirely new genre such as biographies. Or they can always choose from the lively *Toolkit* articles featured in *Keep Reading! A Source Book of Short Text*.

*The following **sample weekly schedule** shows how* Toolkit *teaching might be scheduled into all three literacy models.*

	Instruction	Text Options
Day 1	*Toolkit* Lesson Launch	*PTK* read-aloud or *TFK* poster
	Create a long block of time to move through modeling, guided practice, collaborative or independent practice, and the share session to launch this lesson/practice.	■ Big book for shared reading ■ Selection from basal anthology ■ Your own text—read-aloud, big book, or short text
Day 2	Minilesson to review the *Toolkit* strategy	Review with *Toolkit* text OR review the same strategy in guided reading small-group lesson OR use the same strategy with basal selection
	Kids practice	■ In reader's workshop with self-selected text ■ In a balanced literacy program with leveled text ■ In a basal program with basal text or leveled text ■ With any text you or the children choose
Days 3, 4, 5	Continue brief minilesson review each day. Support kids as they practice based on their learning needs and your assessment of their work from Days 1 and 2.	Review with *Toolkit* text or text you select: big book, short text, story
	Kids practice	■ In reader's workshop with self-selected text ■ In a balanced literacy program with leveled text ■ In a basal program with basal text or leveled text ■ With any text you or the children choose

Assessment:
Teaching with the End in Mind

One wonderful luxury of working with K–2 kids is that, in most states, we aren't directly under the pressure of high-stakes standardized tests. Of course, these exams arrive soon enough—often in third grade—and the scores kids receive as nine-year-olds reflect everything we have taught them from kindergarten on up. But still, when working with five- to eight-year-olds, these looming tests aren't a daily assessment concern. So we can focus all our assessment energy on what really matters for young readers.

All the lessons, responses, and discussions described in the *PTK* have one purpose: to move kids toward independence as readers. What really matters is that they internalize reading and thinking behaviors that promote understanding: activating and connecting background knowledge, asking thoughtful questions, inferring big ideas, and synthesizing information to share it. Authentic assessment informs us about three things: children's learning and understanding, the effectiveness of our past instruction, and where we need to go next. Responsive teaching and assessment go hand in hand. We use the evidence of what we see in students' work to tailor future instruction to their needs. When we listen to kids, watch them closely, ask them questions, and confer with them to find out what they think, we learn not only what they understand, but also what they don't understand. That tells us how to plan further instruction that is responsive to their learning needs.

Kids reveal their comprehension by talking, drawing, and writing about what they read or view. Their responses create a window into their minds. We get to know children well as learners when we pay attention to what they say and what they do. When we let kids take the lead, we send the message that, more than anything else, their thinking matters. We look carefully at children's drawings and writings and realize that our youngest learners may be better able to express their thinking through conversation and pictures. As they begin to write, we support them to use their knowledge of sound/letter correspondence to write their message in invented spelling. We applaud and encourage kids' earliest attempts at responding—knowing that it's what they are thinking that matters.

Assessment Happens 24/7

Continuous assessment of kids' thinking and work is paramount, so after each *Toolkit* lesson there are several pages of kids' responses—created as they worked collaboratively or independently on the strategy we introduced in the lesson. We've included a wide range of responses to demonstrate that five- to eight-year-olds can all notice new learning, ask questions, or infer meaning from a picture. Children are at varying levels of development and at varying levels on the continuum of learning to read and write, so the responses they produce vary. We celebrate this and make sure kids share these responses with each other, as kids are our teaching partners. Often when kids share their thinking in original ways, other kids get the idea and give it a try. Poems on mobiles or animals popping up off posters appear in the classroom. In Reflect and Assess, we weigh in with our comments about each child's work, to share what we understand about kids' thinking and how well they understand what we are trying to teach them. Often we suggest what a follow-up conference with the child might focus on and where we would go next.

We find out if readers are understanding and able to articulate their learning in the following ways:

- We listen to kids.

- We read kids' written work.

- We look carefully at their artwork.

- We confer with kids.

- We observe behavior and expressions.

- We keep anecdotal records of conferences and conversations.

- We script what kids say, recording their comments and questions.

- We use rubrics to keep track of kids' learning, assessing specifically what we have taught and attaching evidence of their learning and understanding to the rubric.

Toolkit Rubrics: From Assessment to Evaluation

Grades are all about evaluating what kids have learned through practice. We evaluate and give grades only after students have had plenty of time to practice and internalize the reading and thinking strategies. When we give a grade, we use a substantial body of evidence that stands as proof of kids' learning. The work samples, drawings, student talk, responses, and artifacts that demonstrate learning are the evidence we use in evaluation.

We look at kids' drawing and writing and listen to their comments in order to use the anecdotal rubrics included in the *Toolkit*. Constructed and more open-ended responses like the examples in the lessons (Post-its, thinksheets, and also posters, poems, and other projects) give us the confidence to know that when we are asked to grade children's work, we are basing our evaluation on authentic learning.

We have designed a series of "annotated rubrics" that support authentic assessment and frame our approach to evaluation. These enable us to move from ongoing assessment to a more formal evaluation of our students' understanding. Each Strategy Book in the *Toolkit* contains a number of lessons that build understanding of a particular strategy over time. The rubrics appear at the end of each book and reflect the kind of thinking and reading behaviors we expect our students to demonstrate after plenty of practice with a particular strategy.

To keep a record of student thinking, we jot notes on the rubric or staple student work to the form. For us, rubric numbers don't stand alone. They mean very little without the supporting evidence of student work and teacher comments. Our rubric forms have additional space for teachers to add reading behaviors they think are important and that they have taught their students. As you fill in the rubrics, use evidence of student thinking to assign the point value to each reading behavior. And keep in mind that we only grade what we have taught and what kids have practiced over time.

We view these rubrics as a place to collect and summarize data from ongoing assessment. We have found that when we put the information about kids' work and understanding on the rubric, we can more easily give them a grade. We don't score every response using the rubric and we don't use rubrics after every lesson. Instead, we tie our assessment to the lesson goals and outcomes. These goals and outcomes are synthesized on the rubric. After completing a Strategy Book, we review kids' responses and work samples that we have collected and use these to score the rubrics.

Master Tracker Rubrics

On pages 69–70 are two forms to help you document and keep track of your kids' learning across the six Strategy Books. We hope you'll use these forms as a starting point for your own adaptations, tailor-fitting them to meet your and your students' unique teaching and learning needs.

Master Tracker: Individual Record

Name _____ Last Updated _____

	Strong Evidence 3	Some Evidence 2	Little Evidence 1
Monitors Comprehension • Pays attention to and leaves tracks of thinking when reading, listening, or viewing • Understands the difference between retelling and thinking about the text • Shares thinking with a partner through discussion • Notices the text and visual features and understands they have a purpose • Uses text features to gain information			
Activates and Connects • Understands the term background knowledge and connects new to known information • Includes nonfiction features in written text and pays attention to them in reading • Makes connections between the text and own life and other texts • Listens to inner voice to make sense of text • Merges thinking with new information and reacts to it			
Asks Questions • Stops to ask questions when listening, reading, or viewing • Jots and or draws questions while listening, reading, and viewing • Recognizes that not all questions are answered in the text • Reads with a question in mind and tries to answer it • Uses a variety of strategies to answer questions— looks at pictures, considers the features, reads the text, and asks a friend Infers and Visualizes • Merges background knowledge with text clues to make meaning • Creates mental images (visualize) while reading, listening, and viewing • Infers and visualizes from features and pictures • Infers the meaning of unfamiliar words and concepts • Reads between the lines to understand information in the text			
Determines Importance • Distinguishes between interesting details and important information • Identifies and codes important information • Paraphrases, putting information into own words to better understand it • Distinguishes between facts, questions, responses in taking notes • Organizes thinking to prepare to share it			
Summarizes and Synthesizes • Merges thinking (questions, connections, inferences) to understand important information and surface key ideas • Puts information into own words without saying too much • Synthesizes big ideas from a collection of facts • Creates ways to write, draw, and share learning and make thinking visible • Responds to and learns from peers and participates in a community of learners			

© 2008 by Stephanie Harvey and Anne Goudvis from *The Primary Comprehension Toolkit* Portsmouth, NH: Heinemann. This page may be photocopied for classroom use only.

Master Tracker: Class Record, Week of _____

Name	Monitors Comprehension	Activates and Connects	Asks Questions	Infers and Visualize	Determines Importance	Summarizes and Synthesizes

© 2008 by Stephanie Harvey and Anne Goudvis from *The Primary Comprehension Toolkit* Portsmouth, NH: Heinemann. This page may be photocopied for classroom use only.

Using the *Toolkit* in Science and Social Studies: Active Literacy Across the Curriculum

When we step into a primary classroom that promotes active literacy, we notice a child sketching the classroom praying mantis as it chomps on a bee caught in its clutches. A small group of kids are gathered on the floor, checking out a giant photograph of a cockroach. Kids pull us over to see a poster of a butterfly they're painting or regale us with poems they've written about buzzing, whirring, chirping insects. Maybe it's spring and time for the unit on insects, but the topic doesn't really matter. Kids love the real world—it sparks their curiosity and sends their imaginations soaring about all the possibilities for exploring it.

Active literacy in the content areas means we integrate comprehension practices and lessons with science and social studies instruction throughout the day and across the curriculum. Daily real-world reading is at the heart of *Primary Toolkit* instruction, and resources include a variety of nonfiction: trade books, magazines, picture books, newspapers, poetry, maps, charts, and online sources. We bring the real world into the classroom in social studies, science, health, geography, etc., and use comprehension strategies as tools for learning across disciplines.

To see comprehension instruction in science and social studies, watch the "Reading, Writing, and Research in Science and Social Studies" slideshow and Brad Buhrow's video on *The Primary Comprehension Toolkit DVD-ROM*.

Creating a Culture of Thinking and Learning

David Perkins suggests that "Learning is a consequence of thinking" (1992). We follow his lead and create a classroom environment where students get engaged whatever the subject, exploring and really thinking about content knowledge as they read, write, talk, listen, draw, and investigate. When kids actively use the knowledge they are learning, they are more likely to understand and remember it.

We believe that comprehension instruction in science and social studies is best delivered in what we call "researcher's workshop." In researcher's workshop, kids have long blocks of time to read and investigate topics and respond by talking, drawing, and writing about them. In this way, they actively use their new knowledge as they share and teach others what they have learned. Just as in reader's and writer's workshop, teachers and librarians teach minilessons, and sometimes longer "maxilessons," particularly when we are teaching a concept or a strategy for the very first time. Many of these lessons come from the array of nonfiction lessons and practices offered in the *Toolkit*. Notice we said "teachers and librarians." When classroom teachers team-teach with librarians, research skills are no longer relegated to a few quick, and often disconnected, sessions in the library. Librarians and teachers work together to make sure those all–important research skills and strategies become tools kids use throughout the day and across the curriculum.

During researcher's workshop, we may focus on topics that are part of a district-mandated curriculum unit. Kids can choose specific aspects of the unit, or umbrella topic, that particularly interest them and have at it. At other times, kids select their own topics. Either approach works. What does matter is that kids are engaged in authentic, experiential, thoughtful practices in which reading, writing, drawing, and thinking serve to build their store of knowledge. These efforts result in diverse, child-authored and -illustrated projects, such as the posters, poems, and student-authored books described in the last two synthesizing lessons (Strategy Book 6). Artistic expression is one of the most powerful ways for young children to demonstrate learning and understanding. Note that the examples included here are simply suggestions: the idea is to give kids much to think about so that they come up with original (and often far more interesting!) ways to share all their new learning. We want classrooms brimming with kids who are enthusiastic, independent learners, so we make sure kids have the time, materials and reading/thinking strategies that allow them to explore their own learning.

Hallmarks for Creating an Environment
for Thoughtful Content Literacy Instruction

The learning opportunities we create

- focus on comprehension and understanding rather than memorization
- connect us with real-world, real-life issues
- center around content-related big ideas, essential questions, and key concepts
- engage students' interest and enthusiasm
- encourage student choice and independent thinking
- provide time for thinking to take place
- set expectations that push students toward higher levels of thinking

When we demonstrate our thinking, we

- illustrate what good thinking looks like
- focus on topics and ideas worth thinking about
- reveal our curiosity, interests, and passions
- explicitly show how we understand what we read through questioning, drawing inferences, synthesizing information and ideas, etc.

We support attitudes and interactions that

- emphasize a common language for talking about thinking and learning
- encourage and respect different viewpoints and perspectives
- ensure that students experience positive ways of thinking about and engaging with content
- spark thoughtful discussion and debate
- support students' enthusiasm for discovery and their readiness to investigate what's new or unusual

Student artifacts and work products

- are the result of thoughtful work and send the message that thinking matters
- make thinking visible
- involve sharing knowledge and teaching others
- illustrate the process of thinking and learning

Materials, texts, and the literature that students read

- encourage a variety of perspectives, opinions, and interpretations
- require students to solve or discover problems
- provoke discussion and raise significant issues
- focus on content-related themes, issues, and/or essential questions

Adapted from *Intellectual Character: What It Is, Why It Matters, and How to Get It* by Ron Ritchhart

A Framework for Reading, Writing, and Research

We developed the following four-part framework to guide lesson design and planning for instruction in science and social studies. Each part of the framework describes what teachers do to guide instruction and how kids engage in these varied learning experiences.

Activate, explore, and build background knowledge

Teachers	Kids	Toolkit lesson link
Connect curriculum topics to kids' interests and experiences	Think about what they know and connect new information to their background knowledge, lives, and experiences	Lesson 1: Think about the Text Lesson 6: Make Connections
Collect and organize materials related to the topic—picture books, artifacts, charts, magazines, and online sources	Explore, experience, and learn about the topic using texts, visuals, artifacts	Lesson 2: Notice and Think about Nonfiction Features Lesson 7: Merge Thinking with New Learning
Immerse kids in topic and encourage questions and responses	Listen, read, talk, view, draw, and write to respond and wonder	Lesson 8: View and Read to Learn and Wonder Lesson 9: Wonder about New Information

Read to learn and understand information

Demonstrate ways to read, view, and respond to information	Read, write, talk, and draw to notice new information	Lesson 7: Merge Thinking with New Learning
Show how to merge thinking with new information	React, respond, and merge their thinking as they learn new information	Lesson 8: View and Read to Learn and Wonder
Model learning from visual and text features	Notice and respond to information from features	Lesson 2: Notice and Think about Nonfiction Features Lesson 14: Make Sense of New Information
Demonstrate how to ask and answer questions	Develop questions and read, listen, and view to answer them	Lesson 10: Use Questions as Tools for Learning Lesson 11: Read with a Question in Mind

Summarize and synthesize information and big ideas

Teachers	Kids	Toolkit *lesson link*
Teach the difference between important information and details	Sort out what's important from less important details	Lesson 16: Figure Out What's Important
Teach paraphrasing. Show ways to summarize information and add your thinking	Put information into own words to understand it. Begin to summarize information in their own words, through writing, pictures, and features	Lesson 17: Paraphrase Information
Demonstrate examples of ways to summarize and synthesize learning	Organize and summarize learning in a variety of ways	Lesson 18: Organize Your Thinking as You Read. Lesson 19: Summarize Information. Lesson 20: Read to Get the Big Ideas

Share learning and demonstrate understanding

Teachers	Kids	Toolkit *lesson link*
Establish expectations for projects and ways to respond to and assess them	Demonstrate understanding and learning through writing and drawing posters, poems, books, etc.	Lesson 19: Summarize Information. Lesson 21: Explore and Investigate
Model possibilities for final projects	Become teachers as they share knowledge with others through projects	Lesson 22: Share Your Learning
Provide opportunities for kids to respond to each other's work to build a community of learners	Talk, write, and draw as they learn from and respond to one another	Lesson 22: Share Your Learning

Using *Toolkit* Components in Science and Social Studies

There are several ingredients that help you integrate *Primary Toolkit* comprehension practices and lessons with reading, writing, and research in science and social studies. These include:

Reading, Writing, and Research in Science and Social Studies

Using photographs of kids at work in classrooms and examples of student work, this slideshow shows researcher's workshop in action. It summarizes general principles for integrating comprehension instruction with curriculum topics. We show how this happens in a kindergarten unit on Africa, a first-grade study of the rain forest, and a second-grade science unit on weather. The four-part framework and practices described here can be used with any topic under the sun. Our slideshow examples come from district curriculum units we've taught in classrooms. The last section of the slideshow demonstrates how children begin to use comprehension practices such as noticing new learning, asking and answering questions, and summarizing learning through drawing and writing as they research and investigate self-selected topics.

Classroom Video: "Content Literacy: Reading, Writing, and Research"

This video with primary classroom teacher Brad Buhrow shows children summarizing and synthesizing information about the rain forest. Kids create and construct a large, three-dimensional rain forest mural in the classroom, adding pictures, captions, labels, and other features of rain forest plants and animals as they learn about them. We also see a small group lesson, observing how Brad supports kids to play with language and create poems about the rain forest. As Brad confers with kids as they work in pairs or on their own during this researcher's workshop, we see how artistic and written expression are powerful tools kids can use to share their excitement and demonstrate their learning.

The Six Strategy Books

Each and every *Toolkit* lesson can be used with science or social studies texts—trade nonfiction, magazine articles, poetry, narratives, you name it. Just as kids use strategies for monitoring understanding, activating and connecting background knowledge, asking questions, etc. in their literacy block, so they apply these whenever they listen, read, and view in other subjects. Over the course of these lessons, comprehension practices become tools for kids as they "read to learn" across the curriculum.

The summarizing and synthesizing strategy book focuses on lessons that teach kids to summarize and synthesize information as part of a classroom unit on the rain forest. Although kids explore the rain forest topic in these lesson examples, these lessons can be used with any curricular topic. The four lessons in this strategy book include how to take notes and record information, summarize big ideas in response to a story about the rain forest, and create projects that synthesize information and demonstrate understanding. As kids internalize these reading, thinking, and writing strategies over time, they become research practices children use to explore and investigate topics they are passionate about.

Keep Reading! A Source Book of Short Text

And last, but not at all least, the *Toolkit Source Book* is chock-full of articles on science and social studies topics from bald eagles to recycling to the amazing Helen Keller.

The Primary Comprehension Toolkit
Research Base

Since you are consulting this section, we assume you are already knowledgeable about the importance of explicit instruction in comprehension strategies. If not, we invite you to consult *Strategies That Work: Teaching Comprehension for Understanding and Engagement* (2007).

The pedagogy and curriculum of *The Primary Comprehension Toolkit* are grounded in scientifically based research studies conducted over many years. Each of the following sections briefly summarizes conclusions and key principles from the relevant research that underpins *Toolkit* instruction.

Proficient Readers Use Specific Comprehension Strategies to Construct Meaning from Text

What the Research Says: Each of the strategies in *The Primary Comprehension Toolkit* is supported by multiple research studies summarized by Pearson, Dole, Duffy, and Roehler (1992) and Pressley (1976 and 2002) as they determined those strategies that active, thoughtful readers use when constructing meaning from text. They found that proficient readers:

- search for connections between what they know and the new information in the text;

- ask questions of themselves, the author, and the text;

- draw inferences during and after reading;

- distinguish important and less important ideas in a text;

- synthesize information within and across texts;

- monitor understanding and repair faulty comprehension; and

- visualize and create mental images of ideas in the text.

What **The Primary Comprehension Toolkit** *Does:* As their titles suggest, each of the strategy books in *The Primary Comprehension Toolkit* focuses on a research-based active reading strategy: *Monitor Comprehension, Activate and Connect, Ask Questions, Infer and Visualize, Determine Importance,* and *Summarize and Synthesize.* The lessons in each book build on one another to give children multifaceted ways to construct meaning. As children approach each new text, they practice another dimension of the strategy, gaining confidence as the unit progresses.

Teaching Multiple Strategies in an Authentic Context Improves Comprehension

What the Research Says: Recent research studies have described the effectiveness of transactional strategy instruction (Pressley 2002; Guthrie 2003). Rather than relying upon a single strategy focus, transactional strategy instruction teaches students a repertoire of strategies that they apply flexibly according to the demands of the reading tasks and texts they encounter. Pressley (2002) found that students who were taught a group of strategies performed better than those receiving more traditional instruction when asked to think aloud about and interpret texts. These findings seem to hold true for younger children (Pearson and Duke 2001) and for students learning information in content topics such as science (Reutzel, Smith, and Fawson 2005). Trabasso and Bouchard (2002) conclude that "there is strong empirical evidence that the instruction of more than one strategy in a natural context leads to the acquisition and use of reading comprehension strategies and transfers to standardized comprehension tests."

What **The Primary Comprehension Toolkit** *Does:* Each of the strategy books in the *Toolkit* focuses on developing multiple aspects of a single strategy—but not to the exclusion of other strategies. The emphasis is on guiding and responding to students' own efforts to get meaning from real nonfiction text—from trade books, children's magazines, and other contexts children are likely to encounter or consult in the course of learning about their world.

Explicit Instruction Within the Gradual Release of Responsibility Model Is Effective in Teaching Comprehension Strategies

What the Research Says: In a research review, Pearson and Gallagher (1983) found that strategy use and monitoring while reading were characteristic of more mature and better readers. The Gradual Release of Responsibility Framework that they outlined emphasized modeling, guided practice, independent practice, and feedback and proved effective in teaching students to summarize an expository passage, ask questions about it, detect difficult portions, and make predictions about new passages. Most important, students eventually assumed responsibility for monitoring these tasks themselves.

What **The Primary Comprehension Toolkit** *Does:* *The Primary Comprehension Toolkit* lessons follow a consistent but flexible teaching approach that begins with intensive teacher guidance and gradually turns the lesson over to the children. **Connect and Engage** opens the lesson by tapping into the students' background knowledge and natural curiosity before moving to **Model**, where the teacher provides explicit modeling of the chosen strategy (or strategies) using the lesson text. During **Guide**, students practice the strategy with guidance from the teacher, who assesses whether or not students are ready to apply the strategy on their own. When students are ready, they **Collaborate** with peers or work independently (**Independent Practice**) to deepen their understanding of the information and ideas in the text. Finally, they come back together and **Share the Learning** as a whole group. Over time, children learn to apply strategies to foster understanding in a variety of genres.

Comprehension Strategies Should Be Used as Tools for Learning Across the Curriculum and in a Variety of Disciplines

What the Research Says: When kids actively use the new knowledge they gain through reading, they are far more likely to understand and genuinely learn it. David Perkins (1992) discovered from years of observations of children in a variety of school settings that "learning is a consequence of thinking. . . . Far from thinking coming after knowledge, knowledge comes on the coattails of thinking. As we think about and with the content we are learning, we truly learn it." Ritchhart and Perkins (2006) and their colleagues at Harvard's Project Zero have concluded from their research that teachers can best cultivate students' thinking and learning by encouraging attitudes of curiosity, mindfulness, and inquiry. They provide evidence that a culture of thinking is created in classrooms where teachers and students use a language of thinking that emphasizes wondering and asking questions, discussion and debate, drawing conclusions, and synthesizing information through talking, writing, and artistic expression.

Another body of recent research views literacy as a tool for understanding in a variety of disciplines, including history, science, and mathematics. Studies by Barber, Catz, and Arya (2006) at the University of California, Berkeley, found that combining scientific exploration and experimentation with science reading in specific topics increased students' acquisition of science content knowledge. Science experiences and thoughtful interactions with science texts also had an impact on students' literacy skills. More information on this extensive program of research is available at www.scienceandliteracy.org.

What The Primary Comprehension Toolkit **Does:** Many of our lessons emphasize reading to learn in science and social studies, building on the research that demonstrates that effective reading comprehension instruction actively engages children in learning in a variety of disciplines. The "teaching language" of the *Toolkit* immerses students in a common language of thinking, learning, and understanding so that the "teaching language" becomes the children's "learning language." Additionally, *PTK* emphasizes the use of artistic expression as a way to demonstrate learning and understanding across the curriculum.

An Active Learning Environment—in Which Curious Kids Collaboratively Read, Write, Talk, and Create—Promotes Comprehension

What the Research Says: For two decades, Fred Newmann and his colleagues have been studying "authentic instruction"—instruction that is highly engaging and interactive, and which connects to students' real lives—and the impact of such instruction on customary measures of schooling, including high-stakes standardized test scores. In two recent studies of Chicago public school students, the researchers found that when teachers offered *less didactic* and *more interactive* experiences, scores on the Iowa Test of Basic Skills rose significantly among a large cross section of students (Newmann 2001; Smith, Lee, and Newmann 2001). Further, in an article reporting results of an NICHD Early Child Care and Youth Development Research study, Pianta, Belsky, Houts, and Morrison (2007) discuss the impact of the emotional and instructional classroom climate on student performance and growth. They conclude that "opportunities to learn in small groups, to improve analytical skills, [and] to interact extensively with teachers . . . add depth to students' understanding." These studies confirm what reading researchers have observed for decades: engaged kids learn more. Allington and Johnston's (2002) *purposeful talk* and Palincsar and Brown's (1984) *reciprocal teaching* emphasize that when students talk about and apply reading and thinking strategies, their comprehension increases. These studies all suggest that kids who thoughtfully discuss and respond to the text more thoroughly process and understand it.

What The Primary Comprehension Toolkit **Does:** In every *Toolkit* lesson, either Stephanie Harvey or Anne Goudvis has meticulously chronicled the ways they engage students' minds and hearts with texts and ideas. Immersed in talk—with each other and with Steph or Anne—kids record notes, respond, build on each other's thoughts, and use thinking strategies to interact with and to understand texts and ideas. The lessons in *Toolkit* are a window into the active learning environment that is every teacher's goal.

Allington, Richard L., and Peter H. Johnston. 2002. *Reading to Learn: Lessons from Exemplary Fourth-Grade Classrooms.* New York: Guilford.

Barber, Jacqueline, Kristin Catz, and Diana Arya. 2006. "Improving Science Content Acquisition Through a Combined Science/Literacy Approach." Paper presented at the American Educational Research Association, April 2006.

Guthrie, J. T. 2003. "Concept Oriented Reading Instruction." In *Rethinking Reading Comprehension*, ed. C. E. Snow and A. P. Sweet. New York: Guilford.

Harvey, Stephanie, and Anne Goudvis. 2007. *Strategies That Work: Teaching Comprehension for Understanding and Engagement.* Portland, ME: Stenhouse.

Newmann, Fred, et al. 2001. *Authentic Intellectual Work and Standardized Tests: Conflict or Coexistence?* Chicago, IL: Consortium on Chicago Schools Research.

Palincsar, A.S. and A.L. Brown. 1984. "Reciprocal Teaching of Comprehension-Fostering and Monitoring Activities." *Cognition and Instruction* 1:117–175.

Pianta, Robert C., Jay Belsky, Renate Houts, and Fred Morrison. 2007. "Opportunities to Learn in America's Elementary Classrooms." *Science* 315:1795–1796.

Pearson, P. David, and M. C. Gallagher. 1983. "The Instruction of Reading Comprehension." *Contemporary Educational Psychology* 8:317–344.

Pearson, P. David, and Nell K. Duke. 2002. Comprehension Instruction in the Primary Grades." In *Comprehension Instruction: Research-Based Best Practices*, ed. Cathy Collins Block and Michael Pressley. New York: Guilford.

Pearson, P. David, J. A. Dole, G. G. Duffy, and L. R. Roehler. 1992. "Developing Expertise in Reading Comprehension: What Should Be Taught and How Should It Be Taught?" In *What Research Has to Say to the Teacher of Reading*, ed. J. Farstup and S. J. Samuels, 2nd ed. Newark, DE: International Reading Association.

Perkins, David. 1992. *Smart Schools: Better Thinking and Learning for Every Child.* New York: Free Press.

Pressley, Michael. 1976. "Mental Imagery Helps Eight-Year-Olds Remember What They Read." *Journal of Educational Psychology* 68:355–359.

Pressley, Michael. 2002. *Reading Instruction That Works: The Case for Balanced Teaching.* 2nd ed. New York: Guilford.

Reutzel, D. R., J. A. Smith, and P. C. Fawson. 2005. "An Evaluation of Two Approaches for Teaching Reading Comprehension Strategies in the Primary Years Using Science Information Texts." *Early Childhood Research Quarterly* 20:276–305.

Ritchhart, Ron, and David Perkins. 2008. "Making Thinking Visible." *Educational Leadership* 65: 57–61.

Smith, Julia, Valerie Lee, and Fred Newmann. 2001. *Instruction and Achievement in Chicago Elementary Schools.* Chicago, IL: Consortium on Chicago Schools Research.

Trabasso, Tom, and Edward Bouchard. 2002. "Teaching Readers How to Comprehend Text Strategically." In *Comprehension Instruction: Research-Based Best Practices*, ed. Cathy Collins Black and Michael Pressley. New York: Guilford.

Master Tracker:
Class Record, Week of _____

Name	Monitors Comprehension	Activates and Connects	Asks Questions	Infers and Visualizes	Determines Importance	Summarizes and Synthesizes

Master Tracker: Individual Record

Name _____   Last Updated _____

	Strong Evidence 3	Some Evidence 2	Little Evidence 1
Monitors Comprehension • Pays attention to and leaves tracks of thinking when reading, listening, or viewing • Understands the difference between retelling and thinking about the text • Shares thinking with a partner through discussion • Notices the text and visual features and understands they have a purpose • Uses text features to gain information			
Activates and Connects • Understands the term *background knowledge* and connects new to known information • Includes nonfiction features in written text and pays attention to them in reading • Makes connections between the text and own life and other texts • Listens to inner voice to make sense of text • Merges thinking with new information and reacts to it			
Asks Questions • Stops to ask questions when listening, reading, or viewing • Jots and or draws questions while listening, reading, and viewing • Recognizes that not all questions are answered in the text • Reads with a question in mind and tries to answer it • Uses a variety of strategies to answer questions— looks at pictures, considers the features, reads the text, and asks a friend			
Infers and Visualizes • Merges background knowledge with text clues to make meaning • Creates mental images (visualizes) while reading, listening, and viewing • Infers and visualizes from features and pictures • Infers the meaning of unfamiliar words and concepts • Infers from text and pictures to understand the story			
Determines Importance • Distinguishes between interesting details and important information • Identifies and codes important information • Paraphrases, putting information into own words to better understand it • Distinguishes between facts, questions, responses in taking notes • Organizes thinking to prepare to share it			
Summarizes and Synthesizes • Merges thinking (questions, connections, inferences) to understand important information and surface key ideas • Puts information into own words without saying too much • Synthesizes big ideas from a collection of facts • Creates ways to write, draw, and share learning and make thinking visible • Responds to and learns from peers and participates in a community of learners			

Works Cited Throughout the *Toolkit*

Atwell, Nancy. 1998. *In the Middle: New Understandings about Writing, Reading, and Learning.* Portsmouth, NH: Heinemann.

Calkins, Lucy. 1994. *The Art of Teaching Writing.* Portsmouth, NH: Heinemann.

Cunningham, Patricia, Dorothy Hall, and James Cunningham. 2000. *Guided Reading the Four Blocks Way.* Greensboro, NC: Carson-Dellosa Publishing.

Davey, Beth. 1983. "Think Aloud: Modeling the Process of Reading Comprehension." *Journal of Reading* 27:44–47.

Duke, Nell K., V. Susan Bennett-Armistead and Ebony M. Roberts. 2003. "Filling the Great Void: Why We Should Bring Nonfiction into the Early-Grade Classroom." Adapted from "Bridging the Gap between Learning to Read and Reading to Learn" in *Literacy and Young Children,* ed. D. M. Barone and L. M. Morrow. New York. Guilford.

Fielding, Linda and P. David Pearson. 1994. "Reading Comprehension: What Works?" *Educational Leadership* 51.5:62–67.

Fountas, Irene and Gay Sue Pinnell. 1996. *Guided Reading: Good First Teaching for All Children.* Portsmouth, NH: Heinemann.

Gardner, Howard. 1991. *The Unschooled Mind: How Children Think and How Schools Should Teach.* New York: Basic Books.

Graves, Donald. 1991. *Build a Literate Classroom.* Portsmouth, NH: Heinemann.

Harvey, Stephanie. 2002. "Nonfiction Inquiry: Using Real Reading and Writing to Explore the World." *Language Arts* 80: 12–22

Harvey, Stephanie and Anne Goudvis. 2007. *Strategies That Work: Teaching Comprehension for Understanding and Engagement.* Portland, ME: Stenhouse.

Harwayne, Shelley. 2000. *Lifetime Guarantees: Toward Ambitious Literacy Teaching.* Portsmouth, NH: Heinemann.

National Reading Panel. 2000. *The Report of the National Reading Panel: Teaching Children to Read.* Washington, DC: National Reading Panel.

Paterson, Katherine. 1995. *A Sense of Wonder: On Reading and Writing Books for Children.* New York: Penguin.

Pearson, P. David. 2006. Keynote presentation. National Geographic Literacy Conference. Washington, DC.

Pearson, P. David and M. C. Gallagher. 1983. "The Instruction of Reading Comprehension." *Contemporary Educational Psychology* 8: 317–344.

Pearson, P. David and Nell K. Duke. 2002. "Comprehension Instruction in the Primary Grades." In *Comprehension Instruction: Research-Based Best Practices,* ed. Cathy Collins Block and Michael Pressley. New York: Guilford.

Perkins, David. 1992. *Smart Schools: Better Thinking and Learning for Every Child.* New York: Free Press.

Perkins, David. 2008 (in press). *Teaching the Whole Game: Seven Principles for Meaningful and Lasting Learning*. San Francisco: Jossey-Bass.

Ritchhart, Ron. 2002. *Intellectual Character: What It Is, Why It Matters, and How to Get It*. San Francisco: Jossey-Bass.

Ritchhart, Ron and David Perkins. 2008. "Making Thinking Visible." *Educational Leadership*. 65: 57–61.

Routman, Regie. February 8, 2007. Keynote speech. Colorado Conference of the International Reading Association. Denver, CO.

Trelease, Jim. 2006. *The Read-Aloud Handbook*, 6th Ed. New York: Penguin.